New+ GET UP TO SPEED

Situational

New Get Up to Speed + *Situational* helps students learn how to speak like a native speaker by focusing on contemporary language usage in everyday situations supplemented with modern facts and cultural notions.

Key Features
- Warm Up Activity
- Useful Expressions
- Key Conversation
- Language Practice
- Role Plays
- Cultural Discussion Questions
- Slang & Idioms

1

CARROT HOUSE

CARROT HOUSE

New Get Up To Speed+ 1 Situational
© Carrot House

All rights reserved. No part of this publication may be reproduced, stores in a retrieval system, or transmitted in any form or by any means without the prior permission in writing of Carrot House.

Printed: First published January 2019
Reprinted July 2024

Author: Carrot Language Lab

ISBN 978-89-6732-291-5

Printed and distributed in Korea
268-20 Itaewon-ro, Hannam-dong, Yongsan-gu, Seoul, Korea

Curriculum Map

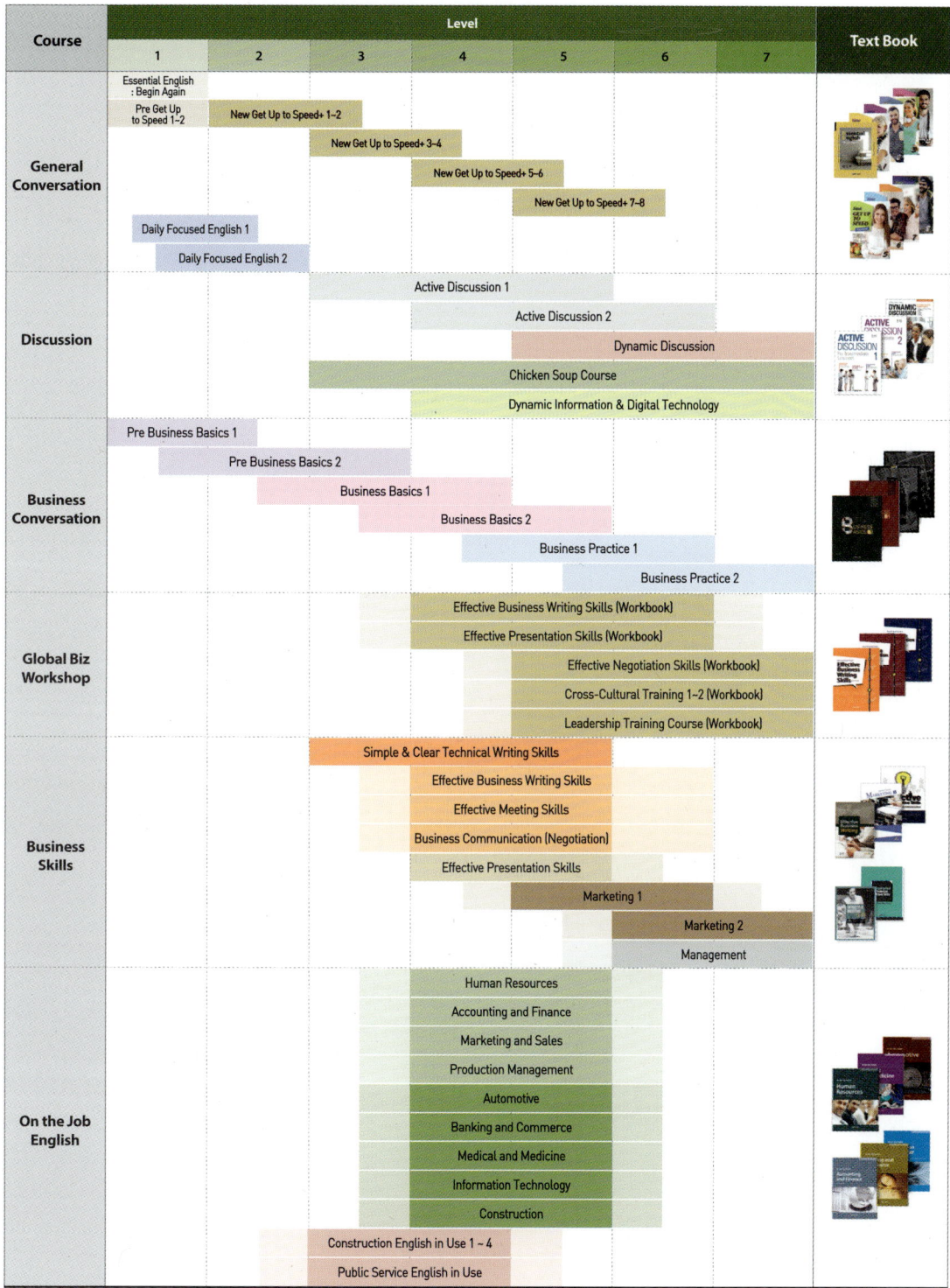

Course	Level 1	Level 2	Level 3	Level 4	Level 5	Level 6	Level 7
General Conversation	Essential English: Begin Again; Pre Get Up to Speed 1–2	New Get Up to Speed+ 1–2	New Get Up to Speed+ 3–4	New Get Up to Speed+ 3–4	New Get Up to Speed+ 5–6	New Get Up to Speed+ 7–8	New Get Up to Speed+ 7–8
	Daily Focused English 1	Daily Focused English 1 / Daily Focused English 2	Daily Focused English 2				
Discussion			Active Discussion 1	Active Discussion 1 / Active Discussion 2	Active Discussion 2 / Dynamic Discussion	Dynamic Discussion	
			Chicken Soup Course	Chicken Soup Course	Chicken Soup Course	Chicken Soup Course	
				Dynamic Information & Digital Technology	Dynamic Information & Digital Technology	Dynamic Information & Digital Technology	
Business Conversation	Pre Business Basics 1	Pre Business Basics 1 / Pre Business Basics 2	Pre Business Basics 2 / Business Basics 1	Business Basics 1 / Business Basics 2	Business Basics 2 / Business Practice 1	Business Practice 1 / Business Practice 2	Business Practice 2
Global Biz Workshop				Effective Business Writing Skills (Workbook); Effective Presentation Skills (Workbook)	Effective Business Writing Skills (Workbook); Effective Presentation Skills (Workbook); Effective Negotiation Skills (Workbook); Cross-Cultural Training 1–2 (Workbook); Leadership Training Course (Workbook)	Effective Negotiation Skills (Workbook); Cross-Cultural Training 1–2 (Workbook); Leadership Training Course (Workbook)	
Business Skills			Simple & Clear Technical Writing Skills	Simple & Clear Technical Writing Skills; Effective Business Writing Skills; Effective Meeting Skills; Business Communication (Negotiation); Effective Presentation Skills	Effective Business Writing Skills; Effective Meeting Skills; Business Communication (Negotiation); Effective Presentation Skills; Marketing 1	Marketing 1; Marketing 2; Management	Marketing 2; Management
On the Job English				Human Resources; Accounting and Finance; Marketing and Sales; Production Management; Automotive; Banking and Commerce; Medical and Medicine; Information Technology; Construction	Human Resources; Accounting and Finance; Marketing and Sales; Production Management; Automotive; Banking and Commerce; Medical and Medicine; Information Technology; Construction		
			Construction English in Use 1 ~ 4; Public Service English in Use	Construction English in Use 1 ~ 4; Public Service English in Use			

※ This Curriculum Map illustrates the entire line-up of textbooks at CARROT HOUSE.

CARROT HOUSE _ 2019.01

New+ GET UP TO SPEED
Situational

Introduction
Carrot House Methodology

Andragogical Approach & Productive English
The teaching of children (pedagogy) and adult learning (andragogy) are distinctively different. Pedagogy is akin to training and encourages convergent thinking and rote learning. It is compulsory, centered on the teacher and the imparting of information with minimal control by the learner. Andragogy, by contrast, is about education as freedom. It encourages divergent thinking and active learning. It is voluntary, learner oriented and opens up vistas for continual learning. Adults need to feel independent and in control of their learning. Therefore, Carrot House curriculum is based on andragogy and is designed to encourage learners' participation and engagement by providing more task-based activities and opportunities to frequently interact in the classroom. People want to achieve communicative competence when they learn other languages. English education in EFL environments has been rather focused on the receptive skills of English—listening and reading—which simply increases learners' knowledge about a language, not the competence of using it. If people are well equipped with productive skills—speaking and writing—they will be competent in English communication. This is why Carrot House curriculum is designed to enhance learners' productive skills throughout the course. This andragogical approach of the Carrot House Curriculum, which focuses on productive English, will enable learners to achieve communication skills necessary for global competence. Carrot House's teaching philosophy and curriculum combine to provide a "Language for Success" for all learners.

Communicative Language Learning (CLL)
This communicative interaction, the essential component of language acquisition, does not occur in a typical, non-meaningful, fun-oriented conversation with native speakers. It occurs in a negotiated interaction through which a well-trained teacher provides the comprehensible input that is appropriate to the learners. The learners, at the same time, actively utilize the opportunities given to them by the teachers. To this end, the Communicative Language Learning (CLL) method is employed in the field of Foreign Language Acquisition. The CLL method provides activities that are geared toward using language pragmatically, authentically and functionally with the intention of achieving meaningful purposes.

Course Overview

Features

Productive English
Learn to use practical and authentic expressions in various daily conversation, common collocations, written sentences, and activities.

Maximization of Schema
The use of visual texts, topic specific questions and useful expressions allow learners to find connections between the contents and their lives by maximizing their schema.

Interactive Activity
Activities, such as role-play, pair-work, group-work, and class-work, provide learners with the opportunity to constantly interact each other.

A Range of Everyday Topics
Through dealing with a range of daily situations in class, learners are equipped to tackle similar situations in reality.

Discussion
Learners can expand their ability to effectively express themselves in English through discussing a broad range of topics.

Slang / Idiom
Through learning topic-related slang and idioms, learners can improve their English language proficiency and use contemporary informal expressions to articulate their ideas.

Opinions on Topic-related Situations
Aims to enhance learner's abilities to speak logically. This task gives learners the chance to express their opinions on a given topic or from a choice of two situations.

Lesson Composition

Each New Get Up To Speed+ Situational book is composed of 12 lessons. Each lesson is composed of 7 main activities and 5 useful extra activities.

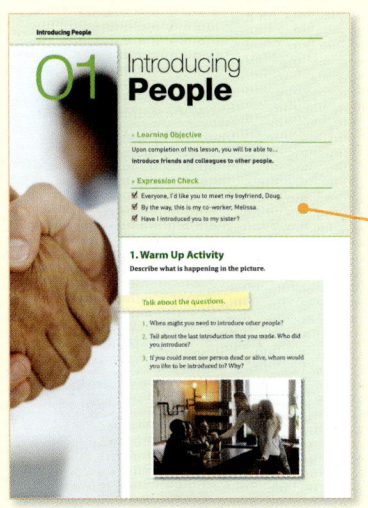

1. Warm Up Activity

To activate the students and their background knowledge, the lesson starts with discussing an image together with three situation-related-questions.

2. Useful Expression

Students can expand their English-language ability by practicing actively used expressions in various situations.

3. Key Conversation

Students can read, listen, and repeat how native speakers communicate with others on a daily basis. The activity also includes questions to test comprehension skills.

4. Language Practice

Students can practice using key words and expressions to complete sentences and create their own sentences. This helps students to apply and remember what they have learned.

Lesson Composition

Each New Get Up To Speed+ Situational book is composed of 12 lessons. Each lesson is composed of 7 main activities and 5 useful extra activities.

5. Role Plays

Task-based role plays puts off the burden of acting but focuses on the language and task achievement and ability to express oneself in various situations.

6. Cultural Discussion Questions

Gives the learners the opportunity to share, learn, and discuss global, cultural, and personal opinions and notions.

7. Slang & Idioms

Reinforce the learner's ability to speak English like a native through the use of situational contemporary slang & idioms.

Extra Activities

Each lesson includes five extra activities: three engaging facts and figures, Situational Collocations, and Did You Know?. These activities provides students with both popular and intriguing global facts. These can also be used to help facilitate a more fun and enjoyable class.

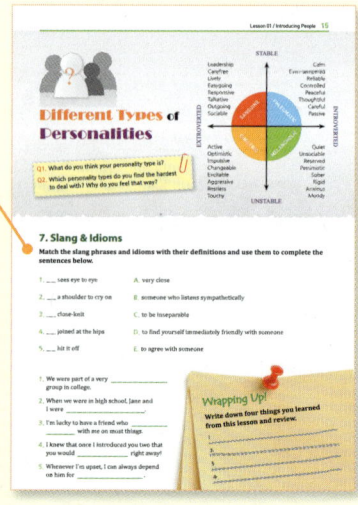

Contents

Title	Learning Objective	Expression Check	
Lesson 1 Introducing People	To introduce friends and colleagues to other people.	- Everyone, I'd like you to meet my boyfriend, Doug. - By the way, this is my co-worker, Melissa. - Have I introduced you to my sister?	10
Lesson 2 What Should We Do?	To make weekend plans with a friend.	- Do you feel like doing something this weekend? - Would you be up for seeing a ball game? - How about catching a movie instead?	16
Lesson 3 Getting a Haircut	To express how you would like your hair cut.	- I just want a trim. - Take a little off the top. - I'm going for a whole new look.	22
Lesson 4 Are You Ready to Order?	To order a meal from a restaurant menu.	- Have you decided what you'd like? - Would you like an appetizer? - Would you like anything to drink?	28
Lesson 5 To Do Lists	To discuss who will be responsible for specific household chores.	- To start with, you have to mow the lawn. - Once you're done with that, the garden needs weeding. - Don't forget to vacuum the living room.	34
Lesson 6 It's On Me	To offer to treat others to a meal.	- This one's on me. - Put your money back in your pocket. - You can treat me next time.	40
Lesson 7 Smart Home Tech	To purchase smart home systems and other smart appliances.	- I'm looking for a new smart home system. - What kinds of features are you looking for? - Do you have any cheaper models?	46
Lesson 8 In the Hospital	To convey warm wishes to people who are hospitalized.	- I wish you a speedy recovery. - I hope you are back on your feet again soon. - You are definitely looking better today than yesterday.	52
Lesson 9 A Tough Week	To talk about a tough work day.	- This has been the slowest week I've had in a while. - It's all downhill from here. - I can't wait for this day to end.	58
Lesson 10 Streaming Trends	To discuss the benefits of streaming services.	- Do we really need another streaming service? - Does it have any unique content? - How many devices can use the service at once?	64
Lesson 11 Budgeting	To create a monthly budget based on your needs and wants.	- We need to set aside some money. - This should be enough to cover the basic necessities. - What's left over for savings?	70
Lesson 12 Calling In Sick	To provide an excuse for missing work.	- I feel under the weather today. - I think I'm coming down with something. - I need to call in sick today.	76

Slang & Idioms — 82

Answer Key — 84

Introducing People

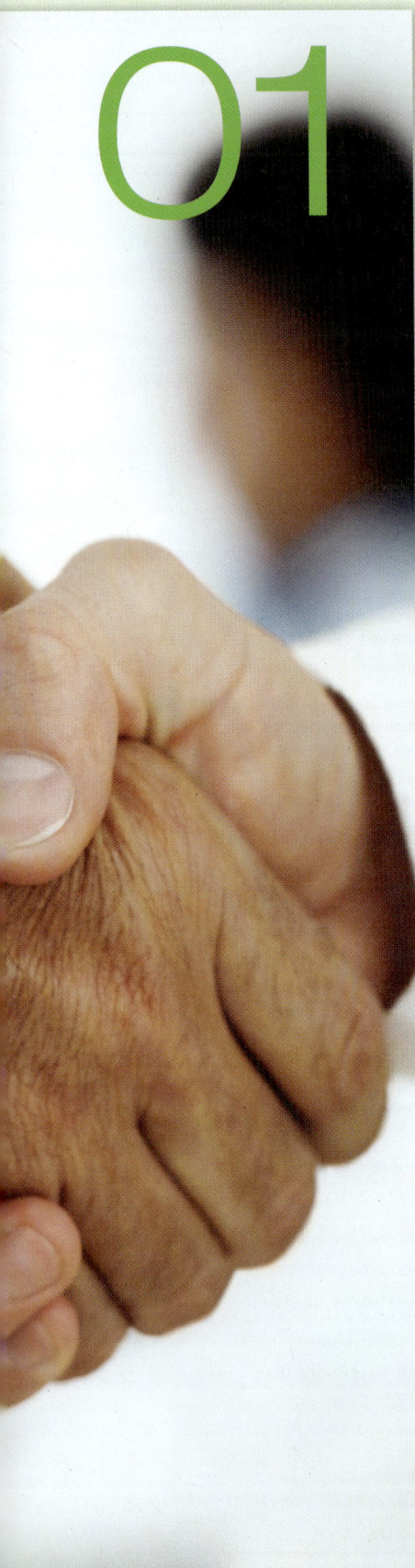

01 Introducing People

» Learning Objective

Upon completion of this lesson, you will be able to...
introduce friends and colleagues to other people.

» Expression Check

- ☑ Everyone, I'd like you to meet my boyfriend, Doug.
- ☑ By the way, this is my co-worker, Melissa.
- ☑ Have I introduced you to my sister?

1. Warm Up Activity

Describe what is happening in the picture.

Talk about the questions.

1. When might you need to introduce other people?
2. Tell about the last introduction that you made. Who did you introduce?
3. If you could meet one person dead or alive, whom would you like to be introduced to? Why?

2. Useful Expressions

Match the expressions (a-d) to its similar meaning (1-4).

A Everyone, I'd like you to meet my better half.

B Let me introduce you to the guy who runs things around here.

C Here's the guy who just beat me at golf.

D This is the person who got me through college.

1 Introducing a former classmate

2 Introducing a fellow competitor

3 Introducing a spouse or partner

4 Introducing a supervisor or boss

3. Key Conversation

Read through the dialogue and practice with a partner.

My Old Roommate

Sam	That food sure smells good, Frankie.
Frankie	Yeah, it's coming together nicely. It should be just about ready. Hey, Sammy, who's the linebacker standing next to you?
Sam	Who, this big teddy bear?
Frankie	Does this big teddy bear have a name?
Sam	Hey, everyone, let me introduce you to the guy who got me through school. Guys, this is Randy Jones, my roommate back in college.
Frankie	Randy, nice to meet you. Anyone who's a friend of Sam is a friend of ours.
Sam	Randy sure helped me out of a few tight spots back in our college days.
Frankie	Randy, you look like you could use a beer and a burger.
Sam	Fix him up, Frankie – and Randy, let's tell the boys a few stories from our college days.

Questions

1. Where do you think this dialogue is taking place?
2. Do the other men know Randy?
3. What kind of relationship do Sam and Randy have?
4. What do you think will happen now?

Introducing People

How Many People Do We Meet in Our Lifetime?

Here is the Secret Formula to find out!

years X 365 days X 3 people = Total number of people I meet

If I am 31 years old:
31 years X 365 days X 3 people = 33,945 people
So far, I have met 33,945 people.

Q1. How many new people did you meet last week?

Q2. Who was the last new person that you met? How were you introduced?

4. Language Practice

Using the key words, complete the sentences then practice making your own sentences.

Practice #1 — Introducing

- my new boyfriend / girlfriend
- a co-worker
- my old friend

★ This is _____ of mine from KJW Company.

★ I'd like you to meet _____ _____.

★ Have I introduced you to _____ from high school?

Practice #2 — Saying hello

- pleasure to meet
- glad to meet
- finally meet

★ Hello, Peter. We are so _____ _____ you.

★ It's great to _____ you all.

★ Hi, Jenny. It's a _____ _____ you.

Practice #3 — Making connections

- talks about / all the time
- have heard / about
- put a face

★ I _____ so much _____ you.

★ It's great to _____ to the name.

★ Steve _____ you _____.

Lesson 01 / Introducing People   13

5. Role Plays

Look at the situations and act out the role plays with your partner.

Situation #1

Role A
You are walking with your parents when you run into an old college classmate. You lived in the same dormitory during your freshman year.

1. Introduce your parents to your friend by name.
2. Tell your parents how you know each other.
2. Promise to call to catch up soon and say goodbye.

Role B
You are meeting a friend for coffee. You run into a college classmate out with his or her parents on the street.

1. Say hello to your friend.
2. Express your happiness about meeting his or her parents.
3. Tell them what you are doing there and say goodbye.

Role A
You are hosting a casual party for your friends at your apartment. You are excited to introduce your new friends to your old friends.

1. Introduce a friend from college to your favorite coworker.
2. Explain how you know each of them.
3. Mention something they have in common to start a conversation between the two.

Role B
You are attending a party at your coworker's house. You are close at work and you are excited to meet your coworker's old friends that you have heard so much about.

1. Thank your coworker for introducing you.
2. Say how nice it is to meet your coworker's friend.
3. Ask a question to make small talk.

Situation #2

Situational Collocations!

Look at the collocations and try making your own sentences.

casual acquaintance	I wouldn't call Brian a close friend, more a casual acquaintance.
mutual friend	I met him through a mutual friend of ours.
keep in contact	We will keep in contact and update the progress.
doing business	I am looking forward to doing business with you.
false impression	I must correct the false impression that I gave you just now.
building relationships	Building strong relationships is essential.
good friend of mine	I want to introduce you to a good friend of mine.
exchanged greetings	The executives shook hands and exchanged greetings.

1.
2.

Introducing People

Interesting Facts About Relationships

1. A study at Loyola Marymount University found that making **eye contact** with your conversation partner might make others see you as more intelligent.

2. In January 2014, the Journal of Experimental Psychology reported that babies as young as nine months old recognize that friends tend to have **similar interests**.

3. A researcher at the University of Liverpool found that men spend **two-thirds** of a conversation talking about themselves, whereas women only talk about themselves for about a third of a conversation.

4. Studies show that remembering bits of information about a person and working them into conversations is not only highly flattering but also shows interest.

5. In 2013, researchers at the University of California found that people look more **attractive in groups** than they do individually. The better-looking people in the group raise the average, making others appear more attractive.

6. Cultural Discussion Questions

Talk about the questions in as much detail as possible.

1. In your country, is it common to call someone you just met by his or her first name? If not, how should you address a new acquaintance?
2. Are there any topics you should avoid discussing with unfamiliar people in your culture? Be specific.
3. In some countries, it is common to shake hands when first meeting someone. How about yours?
4. Tell about a memorable experience you had being introduced to someone for the first time.

Did You Know?

Read and discuss how you feel about each fact.

1. Did you know that more than **80%** of all conversation is about other people?
2. Did you know that it takes the average person just **50 milliseconds** to make a first impression of someone?

Different Types of Personalities

Q1. What do you think your personality type is?
Q2. Which personality types do you find the hardest to deal with? Why do you feel that way?

7. Slang & Idioms

Match the slang phrases and idioms with their definitions and use them to complete the sentences below.

1. ___ vibes with   A. to be in a very close relationship or friendship

2. ___ sees eye to eye   B. to agree with someone

3. ___ tight   C. to work well together, in harmony

4. ___ in sync   D. to have a good understanding or to be on the same wavelength

5. ___ click   E. to quickly get along well with someone

1. We were part of a very _____ friend group in college.
2. When we were in high school, Jane and I were always _____.
3. Her positive attitude _____ mine.
4. I knew that once I introduced you two, you would _____ right away!
5. I'm lucky to have a friend who _____ me on most things.

Wrapping Up!

Write down four things you learned from this lesson and review.

1.
2.
3.
4.

02 What Should We Do?

» **Learning Objective**

Upon completion of this lesson, you will be able to...
make weekend plans with a friend.

» **Expression Check**

- ☑ Do you feel like doing something this weekend?
- ☑ Would you be up to seeing a ball game?
- ☑ How about catching a movie instead?

1. Warm Up Activity

Describe what is happening in the picture.

Talk about the questions.

1. Do you prefer making weekend plans in advance, or would you rather wait and decide what to do on that day? Why?
2. What are your plans for next weekend?
3. What are some things that you do every weekend?

2. Useful Expressions

Match the expressions (a-d) to its similar meaning (1-4).

A Would you be up to taking a walk?

B What are you up to this weekend?

C I can't wait for our weekend getaway.

D I just want to take it easy this weekend.

1 I want to have a relaxing weekend.

2 Do you want to go for a walk with me?

3 I'm excited for our vacation this weekend.

4 What are your plans this weekend?

3. Key Conversation

Think of the useful expressions and practice the dialogue.

Weekend Ahead

Cara	Good morning.
Richard	Hey, Cara. Do you have any plans for the weekend?
Cara	I was thinking of going to the park since the weather looks nice.
Richard	Sounds good! Maybe we can play some frisbee at the park.
Cara	Great idea! We could also pack a picnic and relax under the shade.
Richard	Sounds like a plan! It'll be a nice break from work.
Cara	Definitely looking forward to it. We could use some quality outdoor time.
Richard	Yeah, it's been too long since we've had a chance to unwind outdoors. Should we invite anyone else to join us?
Cara	How about we ask Sarah and Tom? They might enjoy a day out in the sun, too.
Richard	Good thinking. I'll reach out to them and see if they're free.

Questions

1. What are Richard and Cara discussing?
2. Why does Cara want to go to the park?
3. What activity do Richard and Cara plan to do at the park?
4. Who does Cara suggest inviting to join them at the park?

What Should We Do?

Weekend Plans & Weather!

Before making plans for the weekend, don't forget to check the weather forecast. Look at the chart below and discuss what activities are good to do in different weather conditions.

 What might your weekend plans look like if this was the forecast?

Sunny	Cloudy	Rainy	Snowy
• Do Laundry	• Take a Walk	• Watch TV	• Go Skiing
•	•	•	•
•	•	•	•

4. Language Practice

Using the key words, complete the sentences then practice making your own sentences.

Practice #1 — Doing things together
- go hiking / Saturday
- watch / on TV
- go shopping / tomorrow

★ I want to _____ a ball game _____ .

★ Let's _____ on _____ .

★ Let's _____ at the mall _____ .

Practice #2 — Talking about plans
- clean my apartment
- watch a movie
- go camping

★ We'll _____ tomorrow.

★ We're going to _____ _____ .

★ I'll _____ on Saturday.

Practice #3 — Asking about plans
- movie marathon
- having dinner
- go skiing

★ Why don't we _____ this weekend?

★ Are you up for a _____ _____ this Saturday?

★ How about _____ with us tomorrow night?

5. Role Plays

Look at the situations and act out the role plays with your partner.

Role A
You haven't seen your friend in a long time and want to get together over the weekend.
1. Call your friend and ask about how they have been.
2. Ask about your friend's weekend plans.
3. Suggest an activity.

Role B
Your friend calls you to catch up and invites you to do something on the weekend.
1. Let your friend know how happy you are to hear from him or her.
2. Say that you don't have plans.
3. Agree on a time and place to meet.

Role A
Your coworker seems to be having a hard week and you want to invite him or her to do something fun.
1. Ask your coworker about his or her weekend plans.
2. Suggest that you go to a movie.
3. Agree on the movie and suggest you have lunch first.

Role B
You are feeling stressed lately about work and don't have any weekend plans. You want to do something to take your mind off your job.
1. Answer that you don't have any plans.
2. Agree and tell your coworker about a movie you want to see.
3. Decide on a time and a place to meet.

Situational Collocations!

Look at the collocations and try making your own sentences.

national holiday	The office is closed due to national holiday.
long weekends	Extra trains run during long weekends.
make a reservation	I'll call and make a reservation for two.
plan ahead	Book your tickets in advance and plan ahead!
travel abroad	I need to apply for a visa to travel abroad.
well-deserved rest	Hopefully she will receive the well-deserved rest she needs.
worth a visit	If you're staying in Seoul, traditional palaces are worth a visit.
outdoor activities	My family prefers to enjoy outdoor activities on weekends.

1.
2.

What Should We Do?

Do NOT Stay at Home!

What do you usually do on the weekend? If you don't have much time to exercise during the week, try to go out and do some physical activities on the weekend.

Did you know that more than 50% of people are physically inactive in their daily lives?

SUGGESTED WEEKEND OUTDOOR ACTIVITIES

- Jogging
- Playing sports
- Climbing
- Rafting
- Going camping
- Cycling
- Swimming

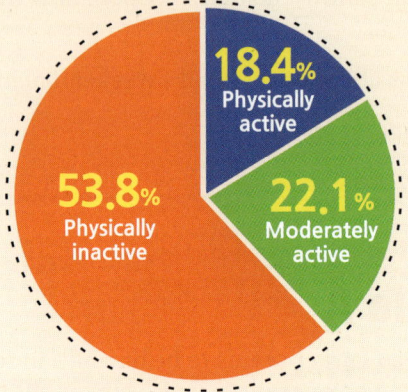

- 18.4% Physically active
- 22.1% Moderately active
- 53.8% Physically inactive

6. Cultural Discussion Questions

Talk about the questions in as much detail as possible.

1. Is it common for people to work on the weekend in your country?
2. How do you usually feel the day before the weekend or a holiday? Explain.
3. What weekend activities are the most popular in your city?
4. Describe your ideal weekend. What would you do? Where would you go?

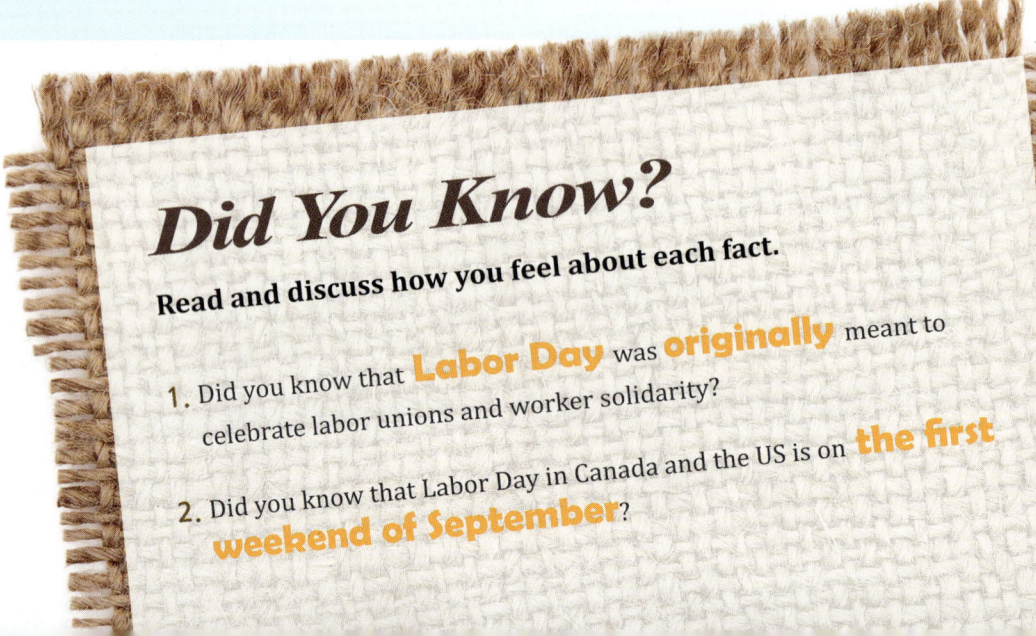

Did You Know?

Read and discuss how you feel about each fact.

1. Did you know that **Labor Day** was **originally** meant to celebrate labor unions and worker solidarity?
2. Did you know that Labor Day in Canada and the US is on **the first weekend of September**?

National Sandwich Day

November 3

It is a celebration of one of America's favorite foods: the sandwich! It is no coincidence that November 3rd is also the birthday of John Montagu, the fourth Earl of Sandwich. This 18th-century English noble wanted to eat his meal with one hand during a 24-hour gambling event, so he instructed his servants to serve him his lunchmeat between two slices of bread. To commemorate the birth of the world's first sandwich-maker, November 3rd is now National Sandwich Day!

Sandwich Day: In some countries, a day between two holidays is called a sandwich day. When a sandwich day comes between two big holidays, then we usually take it off.

Sunday	Monday	Tuesday	Wednesday	Thursday
10	(11)	12	13	14
17	18	19	20	21

7. Slang & Idioms

Match the slang phrases and idioms with their definitions and use them to complete the sentences below.

1. ___ hang out
2. ___ make a day of it
3. ___ tag along
4. ___ short notice
5. ___ grabbing a coffee

A. to devote a whole day to an activity
B. to accompany someone to a place or event
C. having only a brief time to prepare for something
D. to meet to drink coffee
E. to spend time with someone socially

1. I was thinking of going to that concert, too. Do you mind if I _____ with you?
2. I don't have plans. How about we _____ at the park this afternoon?
3. Feel like _____ after work today?
4. It's kind of _____, but do you want to see a movie tonight?
5. I was thinking we could drive to town, do some shopping- you know, _____.

Wrapping Up!

Write down four things you learned from this lesson and review.

03 Getting a Haircut

» Learning Objective

Upon completion of this lesson, you will be able to...
express how you would like your hair cut.

» Expression Check

- ☑ I just want a trim.
- ☑ Take a little off the top.
- ☑ I'm going for a whole new look.

1. Warm Up Activity

Describe what is happening in the picture.

Talk about the questions.

1. Describe your current hairstyle. Are you happy with it, or would you like to change it?
2. When you go to a hair salon or barber, what do you usually have done?
3. Do you often change your hairstyle, or do you prefer to keep it the same?

Lesson 03 / Getting a Haircut 23

2. Useful Expressions

Match the expressions (a-d) to its similar meaning (1-4).

A Take a little off the top.

B I just want a trim.

C I want to get some layers.

D Give me a buzz cut.

1 I'd just like the dead ends chopped off, please.

2 Just shave it all off.

3 I want it shorter on top.

4 Cut my hair at an angle, so it has more body.

3. Key Conversation

Think of the useful expressions and practice the dialogue.

Just a Trim, Please

Prescott What will it be today, Miranda?

Miranda I'm thinking of doing a big chop for the summer. What do you think?

Prescott You could definitely pull off a short, chin-length bob.

Miranda My hair is so flat, though. It might make my face look too long.

Prescott Nah, I'll add some layers to create some body and soften up your look.

Miranda Hmm…on second thought, I think I'll just get a trim for today.

Prescott Miss Conservative. Well, what about letting me add some highlights?

Miranda Yeah, I need something to cover this stupid gray.

Prescott It's not too bad! I think that will freshen up your look.

Miranda Thanks. OK, make me beautiful!

Questions

1. Do you think Miranda is a new client of Prescott's?

2. Do you think Miranda should go for a short cut?

3. Why do you think Miranda doesn't follow his advice?

4. What do you usually talk about with your stylist or barber when getting a haircut?

Getting a Haircut

Hair & Superstition

Every culture has their own unique customs and beliefs about hair. Read the superstitions below and see if you have any to add to the list.

1. Do not wash your hair the day before an exam. Supposedly, it will wash out all the information you learned while reviewing.

2. Do not comb or brush your hair by the window on a full moon it is an invitation to evil spirits, and you may become ill.

3. When a pregnant woman experiences itchiness around her belly, it means her baby will be born with a full head of hair.

4. It is bad luck to cut your hair or shave when a family member is gravely ill or in bad health.

5. Eating corn while pregnant will give the baby long, brownish hair.

6. It is said to be unlucky to have your hair cut when the moon is waning as this will cause it to fall out and lose its luster.

7. Red hair is associated with fiery-tempered people (e.g. Cleopatra and Queen Elizabeth I); black and dark brown hair indicate strength; fair hair implies timidity.

8. If you cut a baby's hair before his or her first birthday, the child will grow up stupid.

9. Cutting your hair during a storm is good luck.

4. Language Practice

Using the key words, complete the sentences then practice making your own sentences.

Practice #1 — Cutting hair

- trim
- a few inches / off
- layers

★ I want _____ taken _____.

★ I think I need some more _____.

★ I'd just like a _____ today, please.

Practice #2 — Coloring hair

- cover up the gray
- adding highlights
- touch up my roots

★ What do you think about _____?

★ Could you please recommend a color to _____?

★ Can you just _____, please?

Practice #3 — Hairstyles

- bangs
- sideburns (male)
- shave the back of my neck (male)

★ Shorten my _____ just a little, please.

★ _____ a little higher, please.

★ Trim my _____ to just above my eyebrows.

5. Role Plays

Look at the situations and act out the role plays with your partner.

Role A
You are a stylist working at a hair salon. Today, you have a new client.

1. Greet the customer and ask what they would like done today.
2. Ask questions about the customer's length and style preferences.
3. Suggest a trim and a simple change.

Role B
You are visiting a new salon for the first time and are unsure whether you trust the stylist at first.

1. Tell the stylist that you are interested in a new hairstyle and ask for their advice.
2. Answer the stylist's questions.
3. Agree with the stylist's suggestions.

Role A
You are a hair stylist who wants to satisfy your customers. You just finished cutting a customer's hair.

1. Ask your customer how he or she likes the style.
2. Apologize and offer to fix it.
3. Ask specific questions to make sure you understand what the customer wants.

Role B
You just got a haircut and you are unhappy with how your hair turned out. Get the stylist to fix it.

1. Politely explain that you don't like it.
2. Tell the stylist what is wrong with your hair.
3. Thank the stylist for redoing your hair.

Situational Collocations!

Look at the collocations and try making your own sentences.

matches well	Your new hair color matches well with your skin tone.
in trend	Bobbed-hair is in trend these days.
new hairdo	What do you think about my new hairdo?
pull out	Could you help me pull out my gray hair?
hair loss	I have recently developed partial hair loss due to stress.
grow hair	I'm trying to grow my hair.
hair extension	I'm getting a hair extension.
messy hair	You will get a messy hair on a windy day.

1.
2.

Getting a Haircut

Very Hairy Expressions

The word "hair" is used in many different expressions, but sometimes has nothing to do with your actual hairstyle.

not a hair out of place

made my hair stand on the end

a hair-raising experience

to get in my hair

pull my hair out

let my hair down

6. Cultural Discussion Questions

Talk about the questions in as much detail as possible.

1. In your culture, is it common for people to change their hairstyle when they reach a certain age? What kinds of hairstyles are most popular in different age groups?
2. Do you always go to the same hair stylist? If not, how do you choose a salon when you need a haircut?
3. Are there spoken or unspoken "rules" for appropriate hairstyles at your company or school?
4. Have you ever gotten a bad haircut, perm, or dye job? Describe your experience in detail.

Did You Know?

Read and discuss how you feel about each fact.

1. Did you know that the average American woman spends *1.5 hours* a week drying her hair?
2. Did you know that *Norway* has the most expensive haircuts in the world? (The average price for a *woman's cut is $95.04* and a *man's is $77.72*.)

Who Are You Talking About?

Look at the picture of people at a party. Then, describe each person's hairstyle.

WORD BOX
- Spiky
- Ponytail
- Bald
- Straight
- Curly
- Shoulder-length
- Bun
- Blonde
- Wavy

7. Slang & Idioms

Match the slang phrases and idioms with their definitions and use them to complete the sentences below.

1. ___ on point
2. ___ off day
3. ___ bed head
4. ___ glow up
5. ___ definite upgrade

A. a positive physical transformation
B. a day when someone doesn't look or feel their best
C. looking very well put-together and styled
D. the messy appearance of a person's hair after first waking up
E. a clear and noticeable improvement

1. I tried to comb through my _____, but I might just wear a hat instead.
2. Have you seen her lately? Talk about a _____ since high school!
3. You should see his new suit for the interview; it's _____.
4. Moving from that old apartment to this new one is a _____.
5. Don't mind my mood this morning; I'm just having _____.

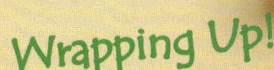

Wrapping Up!

Write down four things you learned from this lesson and review.

1. _____
2. _____
3. _____
4. _____

Are You Ready to Order?

04 Are You Ready to Order?

» Learning Objective

Upon completion of this lesson, you will be able to...

order a meal from a restaurant menu.

» Expression Check

- ☑ Have you decided what you'd like?
- ☑ Would you like an appetizer?
- ☑ Would you like anything to drink?

1. Warm Up Activity

Describe what is happening in the picture.

Talk about the questions.

1. How long does it usually take you to decide what to order in a restaurant?
2. What is your favorite meal of the day to eat out? Why?
3. Have you ever been to a restaurant and not wanted anything on the menu? What did you do?

Lesson 04 / Are You Ready to Order? 29

2. Useful Expressions

Match the expressions (a-d) to its similar meaning (1-4).

A Who's ready for a top off?

B Do you need more time to decide what you'd like?

C Can I bring another round for you guys?

D So, what'll it be this morning?

1 What can I get you this morning?

2 Would you like another drink?

3 Would anyone like a refill on their coffee?

4 Is everyone ready to order now?

3. Key Conversation

Think of the useful expressions and practice the dialogue.

I'm Starving

Waitress	Have you had a chance to decide what you would like?
Chelsea	Yeah, I think I'm ready to order.
Waitress	OK, great. What can I get you to start with?
Chelsea	As an appetizer, I'll have the house salad with the vinaigrette dressing. What's today's special again?
Waitress	Prime rib with roasted potatoes and green beans.
Chelsea	Oh...that sounds so good. I'll have that, please.
Waitress	How about a drink to go with that? Perhaps a glass of red?
Chelsea	You read my mind. Could I get a glass of Merlot, please?
Waitress	Definitely. Don't forget to save room for something sweet. Our chocolate lava cakes are to die for.
Chelsea	Let's just hold off on the dessert order for now.
Waitress	OK, not a problem. I'll be right back with your glass of Merlot.

Questions

1. What did Chelsea order?
2. What kind of a restaurant do you think they are eating at?
3. Do you think the waitress did a good job? Why?
4. Why do you think Chelsea wanted to wait to order dessert?

Are You Ready to Order?

4. Language Practice

Using the key words, complete the sentences then practice making your own sentences.

Practice #1 — Order a meal

- medium steak with a baked potato
- cream of broccoli soup to start
- chicken wrap with fries

★ Could I have the _____ _____?

★ I'd like the _____ _____ .

★ I'll have a _____, _____ please.

Practice #2 — Ask for an order

- appetizer / garden salad
- drink / draft beer
- dessert / fudge brownie

★ A: What can I get you for _____?
   B: I'd like the _____ with ice cream.

★ A: Would you like something to _____?
   B: Give me a large _____ .

★ A: What would you like as an _____?
   B: I'll have the _____, please.

Practice #3 — Choose a restaurant

- new Italian place
- fast food restaurant
- Indian restaurant

★ Let's try the _____ _____ .

★ Want to go to the _____ _____?

★ I'll grab a burger at a nearby _____ .

Types of Red Wine

SYRAH
Pronunciation: Sah-ra or Shi-raz
Food-wine pairing: Red meat (steak, beef stews, etc.)
Typical taste: Aromas and flavors of wild black-fruit (such as blackcurrant)

MERLOT
Pronunciation: Mer-lo
Food-wine pairing: Any will do
Typical taste: Black-cherry and herbal flavors

CABERNET SAUVIGNON
Pronunciation: Ka-ber-nay So-vee-nyon
Food-wine pairing: Best with simply prepared red meat
Typical taste: Full-bodied, but firm and gripping when young

PINOT NOIR
Pronunciation: Pee-no Nwar
Food-wine pairing: Grilled salmon, chicken, and lamb
Typical taste: Very unlike Cabernet Sauvignon. The aromatics are very fruity (cherry, strawberry, plum).

Q1. Do you enjoy wine? Which kinds are your favorites?

Q2. When you eat out, do you usually order a drink? Tell about your favorite drink and what you like to eat with it.

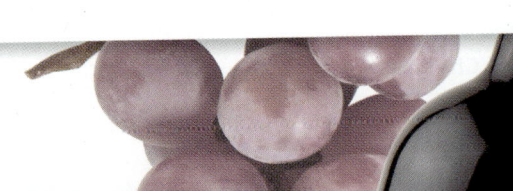

5. Role Plays

Look at the situations and act out the role plays with your partner.

Situation #1

Role A
You are a server at a famous steakhouse.
1. Approach the customer and ask if they are ready to order.
2. Suggest they try one of your restaurant's signature steaks.
3. Ask the customer how they would like their steak cooked and if they want anything else.

Role B
You are a first time customer at a busy steakhouse. You aren't sure what to order.
1. Ask your server for a recommendation.
2. Order a porterhouse steak.
3. Answer your server's questions and order an appetizer and a drink.

Situation #2

Role A
You are eating with a friend at a new seafood restaurant. There are no prices on the menu.
1. Ask the server how much the king crab is.
2. Ask the server to estimate how much one crab weighs.
3. Order the crab and some drinks for you and your friend.

Role B
You are a server working at a restaurant that sells fresh seafood.
1. Explain that seafood is sold by weight and tell the customer today's market price.
2. Give an approximate weight for the crab.
3. Thank the customer for his or her order.

Situational Collocations!

Look at the collocations and try making your own sentences.

strong coffee	I need a cup of strong coffee now.
share similar taste	My husband and I share similar taste in music.
gourmet meals	Every evening, you will be served gourmet meals during your stay at our hotel.
hearty breakfast	We ate a hearty breakfast before starting our trip.
have a craving for	I have a craving for fries and coke.
large portion	A large portion of meat will be served to individuals.
active ingredient	The most active ingredient in these drinks is caffeine.
cut down on calories	To cut down on calories, try using artificial sweetener instead of sugar.

1. ....

2. ....

Are You Ready to Order?

World's Top 3 Most Expensive Foods

Q1. Tell about the most memorable meal you have ever eaten.

Q2. Do you prefer to eat in restaurants or to cook for yourself at home? Explain.

1. Bluefin Otoro Sashimi – $1.76 million/fish

This sashimi is one of the most expensive kind of fish in the market. It is used to make Sushi that mostly served in 7 star restaurants. The Otoro is the most valuable cut of the bluefin's underbelly. Its Omega-3 filled fat melts on the tongue giving a much more flavorful taste than caviar. The bluefin Otoro is prized not only because of its high-grade quality meat but its rarity in the market.

2. Alba White Truffles – $330,000/kg

Also called the "diamond of the kitchen", this rare mushroom is a prized kitchen delicacy. This rare truffle has a deep earthy and musky aroma and very fine taste. Chefs top their dishes with this to greatly enhance its taste. These little mushrooms can only be found by special pigs that smell then deep under the soil. Because of its rarity and difficulty to find, these truffles are auctioned at very high prices.

3. Almas Caviar $35,000/kg

Almas, meaning "diamond" in Russian, is the most expensive and sophisticated type of caviar. This unique caviar comes from the albino beluga sturgeon that lives in the Caspian Sea. These albino sturgeons are very rare, and the older the fish, the more elegant, smoother, and more delicious the taste.

6. Cultural Discussion Questions

Talk about the questions in as much detail as possible.

1. In some countries, it is common for restaurants to make a few special dishes a day that aren't on the regular menu. How about in your country?
2. Do you think that customers should be able to bring in outside drinks and food (ex. a birthday cake or bottle of wine) to a restaurant? Why or why not?
3. Is it necessary to tip at restaurants in your country? If not, do you think it should be? Explain.
4. Tell about the most expensive restaurant that you have ever been to. What did you order? Was it worth the high price?

Did You Know?

Read and discuss how you feel about each fact.

1. Did you know that the average American eats out *4 to 5 times a week*?
2. Did you know that it takes the average person *90 minutes* to eat a meal in a restaurant?

Top 10 Restaurant Chains

1. SUBWAY — The largest chain with approximately 45,000 locations in more than 100 countries worldwide.

2. The second largest private employer in the world and serves over 69 million customers a day.

3. The world's most popular coffee chain and has locations in 76 countries and territories on 6 continents.

4. KFC
5. Burger King
6. Pizza Hut
7. Domino's Pizza
8. Dunkin' Donuts
9. Baskin-Robbins
10. Hunt Brothers Pizza

Q1. Which restaurant chain do you visit the most?

Q2. What is the most popular restaurant chain in your country? What type of food does it serve?

7. Slang & Idioms

Match the slang phrases and idioms with their definitions and use them to complete the sentences below.

1. ___ to-go box
2. ___ bit off more than I can chew
3. ___ to die for
4. ___ can really pack it away
5. ___ worked up an appetite

A. a container used by a restaurant customer to take home leftover food
B. to be exceptionally good or desirable
C. to be able to eat a lot
D. to do something so difficult that it makes you hungry
E. to take on a task that is way too big

1. I shouldn't have tried to make such a difficult dish. I guess I _____.
2. You should try this chocolate cake. It's so good, it's _____!
3. I'm absolutely stuffed. Could I get a _____ for this?
4. You _____! I'm surprised you finished that huge burger!
5. I'll take another piece of pizza. I really _____ at the gym.

Wrapping Up!

Write down four things you learned from this lesson and review.

1.
2.
3.
4.

05 To Do Lists

» **Learning Objective**

Upon completion of this lesson, you will be able to...

discuss who will be responsible for specific household chores.

» **Expression Check**

- ☑ I think we could divide up the chores a bit more evenly.
- ☑ I will take care of the laundry and the dishes.
- ☑ What about cleaning the living room?

1. Warm Up Activity

Describe what is happening in the picture.

Talk about the questions.

1. Do you have a favorite way to relax after doing chores?
2. Which chore is your least favorite? Why do you dislike it?
3. If you could invent a new household gadget or tool, what would it be and why?

Lesson 05 / To Do Lists

2. Useful Expressions

Match the expressions (a-d) to its similar meaning (1-4).

A I have to do the laundry today.

B Could you please go grocery shopping?

C You have to take out the trash.

D Clean your room, please.

1 I want you to buy some food at the store.

2 The garbage needs to be taken outside.

3 Please tidy up your bedroom.

4 I must wash and dry our clothes today.

3. Key Conversation

Think of the useful expressions and practice the dialogue.

All for Today

Melissa	Hey, Daniel. I think we could divide up the chores a bit more evenly.
Daniel	That sounds great. What did you have in mind?
Melissa	Well, I was thinking I could take care of the laundry and the dishes.
Daniel	Okay. What about cleaning the bathroom?
Melissa	How about we alternate weeks on that one?
Daniel	That sounds fair to me. Thanks for suggesting this.
Melissa	No problem. We can work together to make it more manageable.
Daniel	Yeah, that's the spirit! Let's do it!

Questions

1. What does Melissa suggest to Daniel at the beginning of the conversation?

2. Who takes care of the laundry and dishes?

3. What does Daniel think of Melissa's suggestion?

To Do Lists

The UK's Favorite and Least Favorite Household Chores

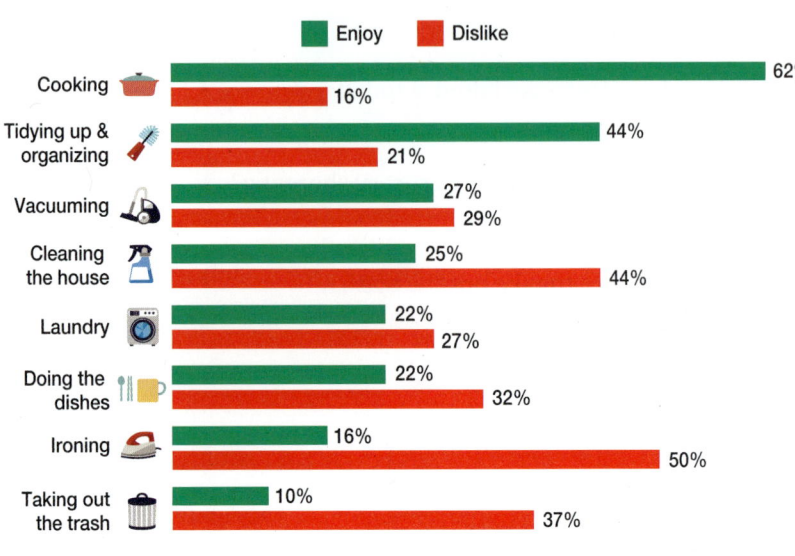

We all have preferences when it comes to household chores – some tasks are simply more enjoyable than others. The chart above shows British residents' opinions about various chores.

Like the graph shows on the right, do you enjoy cooking the most and dislike taking out the trash the most?

4. Language Practice

Using the key words, complete the sentences then practice making your own sentences.

Practice #1 — Asking for help

- clean the living room
- going grocery shopping
- set the table

★ Would you mind _____ _____ ?

★ Please _____ .

★ Can you please _____ _____ ?

Practice #2 — Cleaning

- wash the dishes
- sweep the floor
- fold the laundry

★ I must _____ .

★ I should _____ _____ .

★ I ought to _____ _____ .

Practice #3 — Sequencing tasks

- sort the recycling / take out the trash
- vacuum / mop the floors
- fold the laundry / put it away

★ You should _____ . After that, _____ .

★ You have to _____ first. Next, _____ .

★ You need to _____ . When you're done with that, _____ .

5. Role Plays

Look at the situations and act out the role plays with your partner.

Situation #1

Role A
You are a parent who is trying to teach your child to take responsibility at home. You have a list of chores that you would like him or her to do.

1. Assign your child two chores to do today.
2. Explain how to do the chores.
3. Make your child promise to complete one chore before leaving the house.

Role B
You have plans with your friends but your parent wants you to do chores.

1. Explain your plans to your parent.
2. Try to convince your parent to let you do the two chores later.
3. Agree to do one chore before you leave.

Role A
Your roommate has just come home from work and looks upset about something.

1. Ask your roommate what is wrong.
2. Help your roommate make a list of chores.
3. Agree to do more work because you have more free time.

Role B
Your roommate usually comes home from work much earlier than you and relaxes. When you get home, the house is very dirty and you are too tired to clean.

1. Explain to your roommate how you feel.
2. Suggest that you make a list of chores that need to be done together.
3. Decide who will do each chore.

Situation #2

Situational Collocations!

Look at the collocations and try making your own sentences.

spring cleaning	Our new house needs a spring cleaning before we can move in.
run errands	I've got to run some errands on my lunch break.
burn calories	Did you know that simply doing dishes can burn 120 calories per hour?
do me a favor	Could you do me a favor?
make mess	Kirby is such a nice pet – it hardly makes any mess at home.
do up	I want to do up the house for Christmas.
make yourself at home	Come in and make yourself at home while I finish getting dinner ready.
household chores	It'll take me an hour to do the household chores.

1.
2.

To Do Lists

Time to Fix It!

Use the vocabulary from the Word Box to explain what is wrong with the item in each picture.

WORD BOX
- rusty
- stained
- scratched
- leaking
- moldy
- cracked

6. Cultural Discussion Questions

Talk about the questions in as much detail as possible.

1. In your country, are any chores traditionally thought of as man's work or woman's work? Do you think this is still true today?

2. In the last century, new household appliances have reduced the amount of time we spend on chores. How have chores changed since your parents were young? Explain.

3. In your family, whose job is it to do the following: cooking, cleaning, repairs, and shopping?

4. In some countries, parents make children do chores to teach them responsibility. Is this common in your country?

Did You Know?

Read and discuss how you feel about each fact.

1. Canadian **men aged 25 to 54** spent an average of **2.5** hours per day doing unpaid household work. In contrast, the average **Canadian woman** spent **4.3** hours per day.

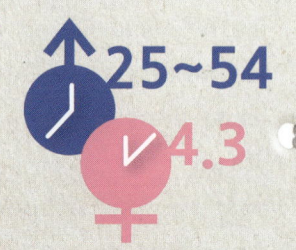

2. The majority of British teens do not participate in household chores. Approximately **75%** have never done laundry or cleaned the bathroom and **35%** have never cooked a meal.

Lesson 05 / To Do Lists **39**

Cleaning Tools
Where and When Do You Use These Tools?

Explain what each tool is, where we use it, and when.

1. Sponge
2. Squeegee
3. Rubber Gloves

7. Slang & Idioms

Match the slang phrases and idioms with their definitions and use them to complete the sentences below.

1. ___ stepped up
2. ___ in my element
3. ___ not my scene
4. ___ keeps it real
5. ___ goes the extra mile

A. not something one enjoys or is interested in
B. stays true to oneself, honest, and authentic
C. feeling comfortable in an environment or activity
D. does more than what is expected or required
E. to take responsibility, especially in a challenging situation

1. I think I'm going to leave. Loud music and crowds are just _____.
2. I trust Jeff because he always _____, even when the truth is hard to hear.
3. Surrounded by other artists, I really felt _____.
4. When her boss was out sick, Jenna _____ to make sure the project got finished on time.
5. Alice _____ to make her boyfriend's birthday special.

Wrapping Up!

Write down four things you learned from this lesson and review.

It's On Me

06 It's On **Me**

» **Learning Objective**

Upon completion of this lesson, you will be able to...
offer to treat others to a meal.

» **Expression Check**

- ☑ This one's on me.
- ☑ Put your money back in your pocket.
- ☑ You can treat me next time.

1. Warm Up Activity

Describe what is happening in the picture.

Talk about the questions.

1. Do you like to treat your friends to meals? Why or why not?
2. When and where was the last time you picked up the tab for a meal?
3. Have you ever regretted offering to pay for someone? Explain.

2. Useful Expressions

Match the expressions (a-d) to its similar meaning (1-4).

A I'll get this one.

B Put your money back in your wallet.

C I'll treat you the next time we go out.

D I'm picking up the tab tonight.

1 I'm going to take care of the check next time.

2 I'll take care of the dinner bill.

3 I'm going to pay for this meal.

4 You don't need to get your money out.

3. Key Conversation

Think of the useful expressions and practice the dialogue.

Put Your Card Away

Annie	Well, I guess it's that time of the day. Shall we get the bill and go?
Suzie	I suppose you are right. The kids will be home from school soon.
Annie	I'm going to pick up the tab for lunch today.
Suzie	No, you don't have to do that. Let me pay for mine.
Annie	Put your card away. I've got this one.
Suzie	If I had known you had been paying, I would've ordered more than a salad.
Annie	Yeah, you sure didn't have very much.
Suzie	Well, thanks for lunch, Annie. Let's do it again soon.
Annie	I'd love to.
Suzie	Sounds great – and it will be my treat next time.
Annie	You got a deal.

Questions

1. What time of the day do you think it is?
2. Why do you think Suzie only ordered a salad?
3. Do you think the bill was expensive?
4. Do you think Annie treats Suzie to lunch very often?

It's On Me

Do NOT Say "Dutch Pay"

"Dutch pay" is not a correct English expression. Although you might have heard Korean speakers use it often, the expression sounds awkward to native English speakers, who use "going Dutch" to describe paying bills separately.

Q1. What is the advantage of going Dutch?
Q2. When do you usually pay the bill for others (instead of going Dutch)?

4. Language Practice

Using the key words, complete the sentences then practice making your own sentences.

Practice #1 — Picking up the tab

- pick up the tab
- take care of the check
- dinner is on me

★ _____ tonight.

★ Let me _____ _____ .

★ I'm going to _____ _____ for lunch.

Practice #2 — Treating others

- lunch / dinner / me
- last week / tonight
- yesterday / this morning

★ You paid _____ , so it's my turn to buy you dinner _____ .

★ You treated me to coffee _____ , so it's on me _____ .

★ You picked up the check for _____ , so _____ is on _____ .

Practice #3 — Confirming

- treat me
- got it
- took care of the bill

★ You _____ last time, right?

★ Didn't you _____ last time we had lunch?

★ Was it you who _____ _____ last Thursday?

5. Role Plays

Look at the situations and act out the role plays with your partner.

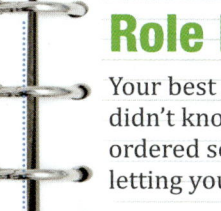

Situation #1

Role A
You invited your best friend to dinner at a nice restaurant. You just got a promotion at work and want to celebrate.

1. Tell your friend that you are paying.
2. Insist that you want to pay.
3. Say it's not a problem.

Role B
Your best friend invited you to dinner. You didn't know he or she was paying, so you ordered something expensive. You feel bad letting your friend pay.

1. Offer to split the check.
2. Thank your friend and accept his or her offer.
3. Promise to pay next time.

Situation #2

Role A
You are eating lunch with your coworker and you each want to pay for your own meal.

1. Call over the server.
2. Ask the server if he or she can split the check.
3. Thank the server and say you will be paying with two separate cards.

Role B
You are a server at a restaurant.

1. Ask what the customer wants.
2. Say that you can do it and ask how the customers want to pay.
3. Tell the customer that you will be right back.

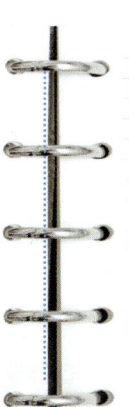

Situational Collocations!

Look at the collocations and try making your own sentences.

have the bill	Could I have the bill, please?
wining and dining	The firm spent thousands wining and dining potential clients.
fancy restaurant	My date brought me to a fancy restaurant for dinner.
big deal	It's not a big deal, dinner is on me.
night out	You deserve a night out with your friends.
blind date	I blew my blind date yesterday.
special occasion	We would like to celebrate the special occasion.
complimentary drinks	He likes to send out complimentary drinks on his birthday.

1. ....
2. ....

It's On Me

Who Should Pay on the First Date?

- 🟥 Go Dutch
- 🟩 Man Pays
- 🟧 Whoever suggested the date
- 🟦 Others

According to a survey, more than half of British women pay for themselves on a first date, even though men still want to pay.

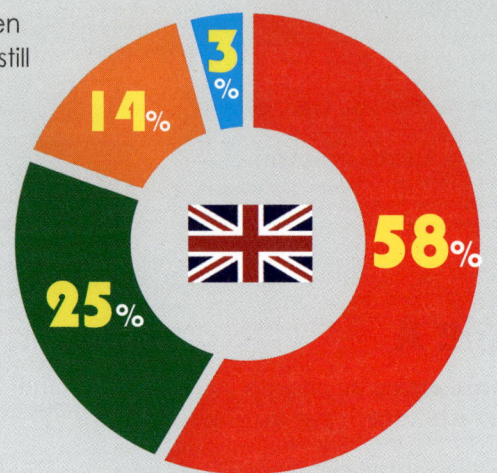

- Q1. On a first date, are you willing to pay for the meal?
- Q2. Do you agree that men should pay for the meal on a first date?

6. Cultural Discussion Questions

Talk about the questions in as much detail as possible.

1. Are there any customs in your country about picking up the tab for food and drinks?
2. In your country, is it more common for men to pay on dates or for couples to go Dutch?
3. In your culture, is it rude to refuse someone's offer to pay for your meal? Explain.
4. With groups of friends you meet often, do you keep track of who pays for what? How do you decide who pays?

Did You Know?

Read and discuss how you feel about each fact.

1. Did you know that **68%** of men treat a woman to dinner on the first date in the US?
2. Did you know **57%** of younger women always offer to pay on the first date? However, 34% of them are bothered if a man accepts, and 46% are bothered if he refuses.

♂ **68%**
♀ **57%**

Lesson 06 / It's On Me

"Could I get a doggie bag?"

A doggie bag is a container provided by a restaurant to customers who want to take their leftover food home. The container might be provided directly to the customer or the server may offer to package the food in the kitchen.

Q1. Have you ever asked for a doggie bag after a meal?

Q2. Do you often eat leftovers or do you prefer to cook another meal from scratch?

7. Slang & Idioms

Match the slang phrases and idioms with their definitions and use them to complete the sentences below.

1. ___ separate checks
2. ___ got yours
3. ___ split the check
4. ___ settle up
5. ___ good for it

A. to divide up a bill
B. to pay what's owed
C. individual bills for each customer in a group
D. can be trusted to repay a debt
E. to cover someone else's portion of a bill

1. Don't worry about the movie ticket. I've _____ since you paid for dinner.
2. I don't have cash now. Let's _____ the next time we meet.
3. I told the waiter we wanted to pay with _____ in advance.
4. Don't worry about lending Greg the money; he's _____.
5. Let's _____ to keep it fair for everyone.

Wrapping Up!
Write down four things you learned from this lesson and review.

Smart Home Tech

Smart Home Tech

» Learning Objective

Upon completion of this lesson, you will be able to...

purchase smart home systems and other smart appliances.

» Expression Check

- ☑ I'm looking for a new smart home system.
- ☑ What kinds of features are you looking for?
- ☑ Do you have any cheaper models?

1. Warm Up Activity

Describe what is happening in the picture.

Talk about the questions.

1. Do you own any smart appliances? Which features are important to you?
2. What are the pros of a smart home system? Are there any cons?
3. Do you prefer to purchase the newest model of something or would you rather save money by buying an older model? Explain.

2. Useful Expressions

Match the expressions (a-d) to its similar meaning (1-4).

A. Does it have any security features?

B. Do the smart plugs work with any appliance?

C. Can we automate other appliances?

D. What are the benefits of a smart refrigerator?

1. How do smart refrigerators make life easier?

2. Can other home devices also be programmed to work automatically?

3. Will it make our home safer?

4. Can all appliances be plugged into it?

3. Key Conversation

 **Think of the useful expressions and practice the dialogue.**

Does It Come With a Warranty?

Salesman	Hello, sir. Is there anything I can help you with?
Steve	Yes, I'm looking for a new washer.
Salesman	What kinds of features are you looking for?
Steve	I don't really know. It's a housewarming gift for my daughter, and I don't know much about these new smart appliances.
Salesman	Well, this model is very popular. It has all the latest features.
Steve	It's expensive, too. I don't know if I can afford it.
Salesman	That's no problem. We do have some older models if you are interested.
Steve	Do you have any models that are more energy-efficient?
Salesman	Yes, we do. This one is very energy-efficient, and it has a variety of smart features.
Steve	It looks perfect! Does it come with a warranty?
Salesman	Yes, we offer a ten-year warranty for it.
Steve	Great! I'll take it.

Questions

1. What is Steve shopping for?
2. Do you think this is a big purchase for Steve?
3. Why doesn't Steve like the first model?
4. What might the salesman say next?

Smart Home Tech

5 Things to Think About When Buying a Smart Appliance

What's the most important factor for you when buying a new appliance? Why?

Price — What is your budget, and which appliances offer the best value?

Energy Efficiency — Which model offers the best energy savings?

Functionality — What features does the appliance provide?

Connectivity — How does the appliance connect to the internet? Via Wi-Fi or a smartphone app?

User Interface — Is it easy to use? Can you control the appliance through a smartphone app?

4. Language Practice

Using the key words, complete the sentences then practice making your own sentences.

Practice #1 — Buying Appliances

- voice-activated lights
- robot vacuum cleaner
- smart plugs

★ I'm in the market for a new _____ .

★ I'm looking to buy _____ _____ .

★ Do you have any _____ in stock?

Practice #2 — Comparing Appliances

- smart refrigerator
- smart home system
- user interface

★ This _____ has higher energy efficiency ratings than the first one.

★ This _____ is much easier to install than the others I looked at.

★ The _____ of this app is much more intuitive.

Practice #3 — Asking About Features

- battery
- larger display
- second security camera

★ How much is it for the one with the _____?

★ How much does a _____ _____ cost?

★ How long does the _____ last on a full charge?

5. Role Plays

Look at the situations and act out the role plays with your partner.

Situation #1

Role A

You are a salesperson in the electronics department. Your store just got a shipment of new 85-inch smart TVs with surround sound and OLED screens.

1. Ask the customer if they need help.
2. Find out what product the customer is interested in.
3. Recommend a smart TV to the customer.

Role B

You are interested in purchasing a new smart TV with a large screen and surround sound.

1. Explain that you are looking for a new TV.
2. Tell what features you are looking for and ask for a recommendation.
3. Ask about the price and other functions.

Situation #2

Role A

You and your spouse are shopping for a new dishwasher. You want one with all the new features.

1. Point out the smart dishwasher.
2. Talk about the benefits, such as energy usage tracking.
3. Highlight the long-term savings on water and energy.

Role B

Your spouse shows you a very expensive smart dishwasher. You don't think you need smart features. You want more information about it.

1. Point out the high price.
2. Ask why the smart dishwasher is better.
3. Say you need to research it more.

Situational Collocations!

Look at the collocations and try making your own sentences.

operate remotely	You can operate the lights remotely through a mobile app.
updated features	The app constantly adds updated features to improve user satisfaction.
cutting-edge design	The car company is known for incorporating cutting-edge designs.
install equipment	The technician will install the smart doorbell equipment in your home today.
navigate the app	You can easily navigate the app to change the settings.
reasonable price	Where can I find office supplies online for a reasonable price?
extended warranty protection	The company provides customers with the option to add extended warranty protection.
run smoothly	The app is designed to run smoothly on both Android and iOS devices.

1.
2.

Smart Home Tech

The Future Trends of Smart Home Tech

✅ **1. Expanded Application of Artificial Intelligence (AI):**
AI technology will continue to advance, learning user habits and environments to provide personalized services.

✅ **2. Enhanced Security and Privacy Measures:**
Introduction of new security technologies and standardized protocols will ensure the safety of user data and minimize vulnerabilities in smart home systems.

✅ **3. Emphasis on Energy Efficiency and Sustainability:**
Increased integration of solar power systems, use of recyclable materials will underscore the focus on energy efficiency and sustainability.

Are there specific functionalities of smart home devices that you are most excited about?

6. Cultural Discussion Questions

Talk about the questions in as much detail as possible.

1. How important are energy-efficient appliances to you? Why?

2. What's the 'must-have' smart appliance in your country? Why is it so popular?

3. Do people in your country prefer to buy domestic or imported appliances? Why?

4. Which smart appliances interest you the most?

Did You Know?

Read and discuss how you feel about each fact.

1. Did you know that the *first smart home device was created in 1966*? The ECHO IV could control clocks and manage air conditioning.

2. Did you know that **62% of Gen Z** renters prioritize smart home tech when choosing where to live?

Smart Home Essentials

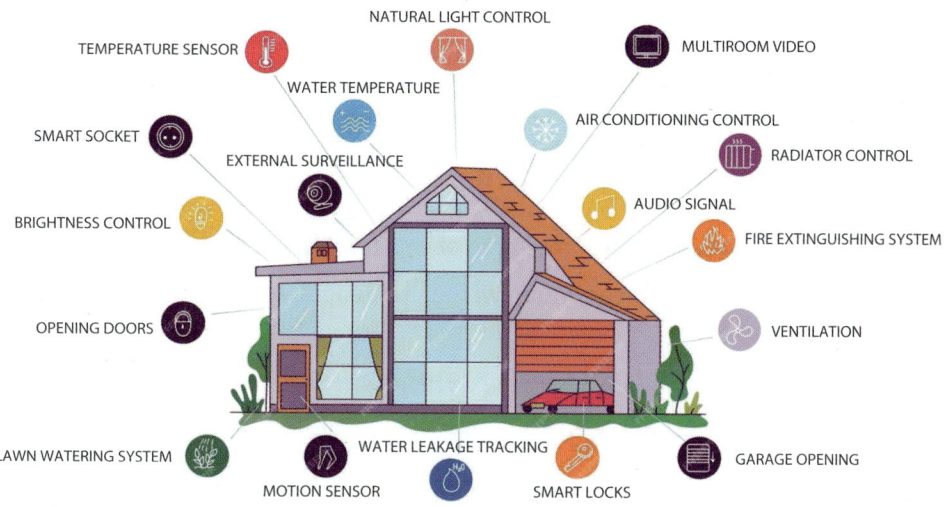

Q1. In your opinion, which smart home features are most useful?
Q2. How can smart home technology increase your home's value?

7. Slang & Idioms

Match the slang phrases and idioms with their definitions and use them to complete the sentences below.

1. ___ go dark
2. ___ sync up
3. ___ hard reset
4. ___ digital detox
5. ___ doomscrolling

A. to link data across devices or accounts
B. returning a device to its original factory settings
C. a period of time when a person stops using electronic devices
D. obsessively checking for updates with the expectation that the news will be bad
E. when someone is not reachable via electronic means or social media

1. If your phone keeps freezing, you might need to do a _____.

2. I'm planning a _____ over the weekend, just to clear my head.

3. Every day, I _____ my fitness tracker with my phone to monitor my activities.

4. After spending hours _____, I put down my phone and went for a walk.

5. Diane warned us she's going to _____ from social media to study for her test.

Wrapping Up!
Write down four things you learned from this lesson and review.

1.
2.
3.
4.

In the Hospital

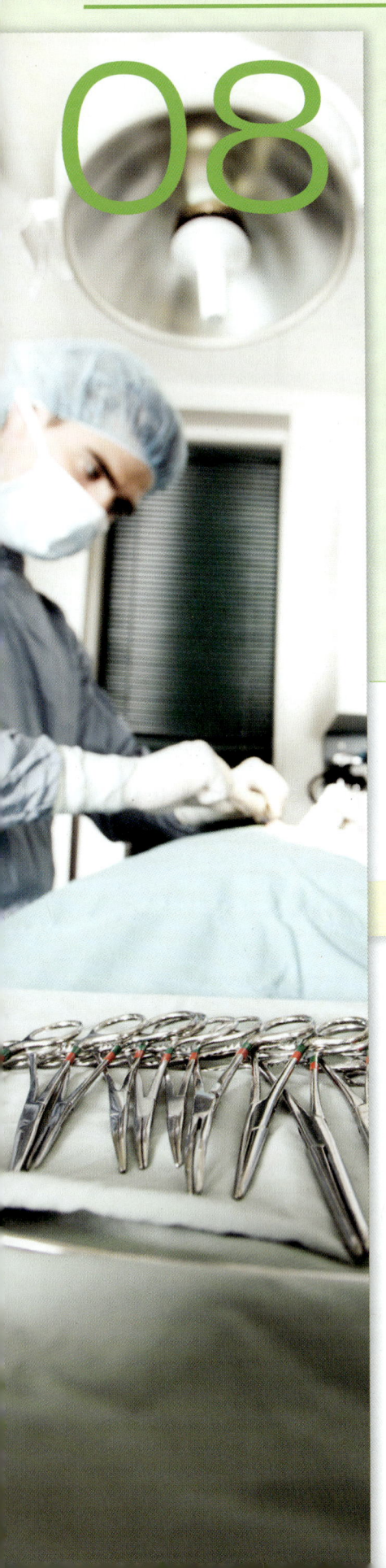

08 In the **Hospital**

» Learning Objective

Upon completion of this lesson, you will be able to...

convey warm wishes to people who are hospitalized.

» Expression Check

- ☑ I wish you a speedy recovery.
- ☑ I hope you are back on your feet again soon.
- ☑ You are definitely looking better today than yesterday.

1. Warm Up Activity

Describe what is happening in the picture.

Talk about the questions.

1. Have you ever visited someone in the hospital?
2. What kind of things might be good to bring to a friend in the hospital?
3. If you were in the hospital, would you like to have visitors?

2. Useful Expressions

Match the expressions (a-d) to its similar meaning (1-4).

A. I wish you a speedy recovery.

B. I hope you are back on your feet again soon.

C. You look like you're on the up and up.

D. So, any word on the diagnosis?

1. Do they have any idea what's wrong with you yet?

2. I hope you feel better and can get back to your normal routine quickly.

3. I hope you get well soon.

4. You are definitely looking better today than yesterday.

3. Key Conversation

Read through the dialogue and practice with a partner.

I Hope You Get Well Soon

David Good morning, sunshine. You are definitely looking better today than you did yesterday.

Rose Hi, David. Wow, thanks for visiting me.

David I came as soon as I heard. How have they been treating you?

Rose It's been all right, I guess. The food is mediocre at best, and this bed is killing my back, but what can I do?

David Can I make you more comfortable?

Rose Well, I could use another pillow. Thanks.

David Do they have any idea what's wrong with you yet?

Rose They're running a few more tests this morning on my stomach, and I should know something by the evening.

David The guys at the office hope you have a speedy recovery and are on your feet again soon.

Rose Please tell them I appreciate their kind thoughts.

Questions

1. What do you think is the relationship between David and Rose?

2. Do you think Rose is happy to see David?

3. Has Rose enjoyed her stay at the hospital so far?

4. Should Rose's co-workers have come to visit her, too?

In the Hospital

Symptoms: Cause & Effect

Look at the pictures and guess which symptoms each person will be likely to experience.

WORD BOX
- dizzy
- headache
- nauseous
- muscle ache
- cold sweat
- cramps
- feeling cold
- high fever
- feeling shaky
- stiffness
- sneezing
- stomachache
- fast heart beat

What do you think will happen to them?

4. Language Practice

Using the key words, complete the sentences then practice making your own sentences.

Practice #1 — Encouraging
- recovery soon
- back on your feet before long
- looking / better / last weekend

★ Hoping you're _____ _____.

★ Praying for a full _____ _____.

★ You're _____ much _____ than you were _____.

Practice #2 — Asking about conditions
- diagnosis
- discharged
- recovery period

★ What's your _____ _____ looking like?

★ What's the _____?

★ Do you know when you'll be _____?

Practice #3 — Conveying well-wishes
- coworkers / get well
- classmates / on the up and up
- wishes he could be here

★ Your brother _____ _____ and he sent a card for you.

★ Our _____ hope you _____ soon.

★ Your _____ say they hope you're _____.

5. Role Plays

Look at the situations and act out the role plays with your partner.

Situation #1

Role A
You are visiting your best friend in the hospital.
1. Find out what sickness your friend has.
2. Ask how he/she feels about hospital environment.
3. Offer to make your friend feel more comfortable.

Role B
You have been hospitalized for food poisoning and you're best friend is visiting.
1. Thank your friend for visiting.
2. Share your diagnosis.
3. You like/don't like the food, but would like something else that will make you feel much better.

Situation #2

Role B
You are visiting a family member who has been in the hospital for a week. He/she needs some encouragement.
1. Ask how he/she feels and cheer him/her up.
2. Give a brief explanation of what and another family member has been doing.
3. Help plan an exciting family trip/event.

Role A
You have been hospitalized for a week for stomach problems. You are feeling sad that you are away from your family.
1. Explain on how different you feel today compared to few days ago.
2. Ask for updates on what your family has been doing.
3. Make plans of what you want to do when you are discharged.

Situational Collocations!

Look at the collocations and try making your own sentences.

balanced diet	You should keep a balanced diet.
serious illness	A cold is not a serious illness.
full recovery	The patient has made full recovery.
contracted (sickness)	My friend contracted malaria while visiting India.
suffered from	My grandmother has suffered from asthma all her life.
diagnosed with	She was diagnosed with cancer.
sharp pain	The sudden sharp pain made me shout.
severe migraine	I have a severe migraine.

1.
2.

In the Hospital

as white as a ghost

Do I look white?

If someone looks white because he/she is ill, frightened, or shocked, we usually use the phrase "as white as a ghost" to describe the person. Learn more about this type of phrase, called an idiom, by filling in the blanks below.

WORD BOX a mouse / a beet / rain / a cucumber / a sheet

1. In math class, he became as quiet as ....
2. He's the calmest person I know. He's as cool as ....
3. You don't look very well. You've gone as white as ....
4. At the party, he was very embarrassed. His face was as red as ....
5. The doctor told me that I'll be as right as .... after I take my pills.

Answer Key: ① a mouse ② a cucumber ③ a sheet ④ a beet ⑤ rain

6. Cultural Discussion Questions
Talk about the questions in as much detail as possible.

1. Some countries have limited visiting hours, while others are 24/7. What rules does your country follow and what do you think is better?
2. Is it appropriate to ask specific questions about a person's medical condition in your culture?
3. How much help does a person usually need from family and friends when someone is hospitalized in your country?
4. Most Western countries promote and embrace mental health care and counselling, while some countries consider it a taboo. What do you think?

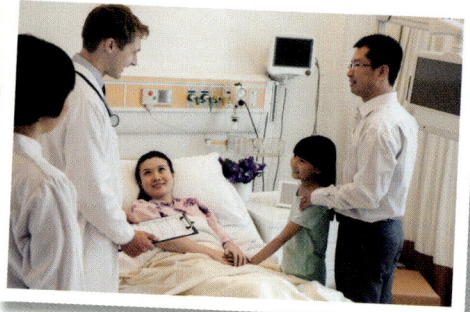

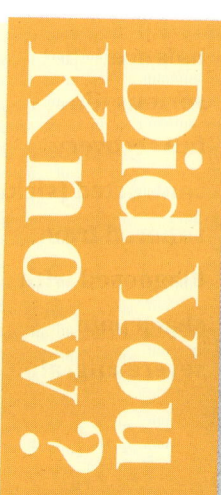

Did You Know?

Read and discuss how you feel about each fact.

1. Did you know that in the US it is considered best to *limit* your hospital visit to *20 minutes*?
2. Did you know that in the USA gifts such as flowers, robes, books, movies, and lip balm are *preferable gifts* for *hospitalized patients*?

What is mHealth?

mHealth or *mobile health* is a term used for medical care supported by mobile devices.

Top mHealth Downloads

- Weight loss — 50 million
- Exercise — 26.5 million
- Women's Health — 10.5 million
- Sleep & Meditation — 8 million
- Pregnancy — 7.5 million

Weight and exercise apps are the most popular types.

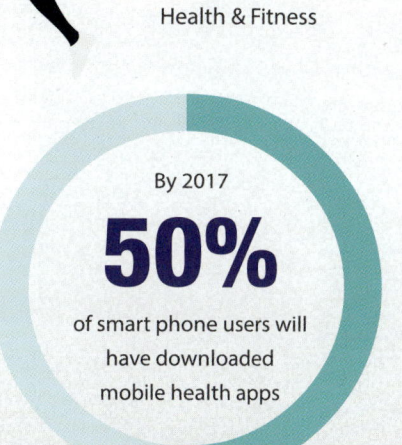

There are over **97,000+** mobile apps related to Health & Fitness

By 2017 **50%** of smart phone users will have downloaded mobile health apps

7. Slang & Idioms

Match the slang phrases and idioms with their definitions and use them to complete the sentences below.

1. ___ runs in the family
2. ___ come down with
3. ___ clean bill of health
4. ___ fighting off something
5. ___ in the clear

A. recovering from an illness
B. to be hereditary
C. no longer affected by or at risk of a particular illness
D. to begin to suffer from an illness
E. fit and healthy

1. The doctor has given me a _____. I'll be back at work tomorrow.
2. I feel like I'm _____ and need to rest.
3. The tests came back negative, so it looks like I'm _____.
4. Unfortunately, diabetes _____.
5. I have _____ the flu, so I can't work today.

Wrapping Up!

Write down four things you learned from this lesson and review.

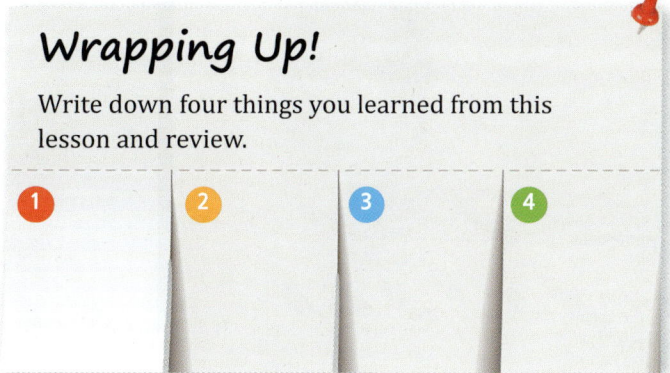

A Tough Week

09 A Tough **Week**

» Learning Objective

Upon completion of this lesson, you will be able to...
talk about a tough work day.

» Expression Check

- ☑ This has been the slowest week I've had in a while.
- ☑ It's all downhill from here.
- ☑ I can't wait for this day to end.

1. Warm Up Activity

Describe what is happening in the picture.

Talk about the questions.

1. Do you feel that your weeks go by quickly or slowly? Explain.
2. What is the toughest day of the week for you? Why?
3. What is the easiest day of the week for you? Why?

2. Useful Expressions

Match the expressions (a-d) to its similar meaning (1-4).

- **A** It's hump day.
- **B** Is this day ever going to end?
- **C** I feel like knocking off early today.
- **D** The rest of the week is all downhill from here.

- **1** I'm in the mood to go home early.
- **2** The remaining days of the week will be easy.
- **3** It's the middle of the week.
- **4** When is this day going to be finished?

3. Key Conversation

🎧 Think of the useful expressions and practice the dialogue.

WHAT A DAY!!

Sally	Oh, hi Sherman. How's your day going?
Sherman	Well, considering it's hump day, it's not going too badly. How's your day?
Sally	Not as good as yours. I can't wait for this day to end.
Sherman	What happened?
Sally	My boss is getting me to do one thing after another.
Sherman	You know, we all have those days. Keep your head up.
Sally	Yeah, I know. I just wish I could knock off early and end this day.
Sherman	Hang in there. Hump day is almost finished, and it's all downhill from here.
Sally	I can't wait for the weekend.
Sherman	Neither can I.

Questions

1. Do you think Sally enjoys her job?
2. Why is Sally having a bad day?
3. Do you think Sherman is a friendly co-worker?
4. What advice would you give Sally if you were her co-worker?

A Tough Week

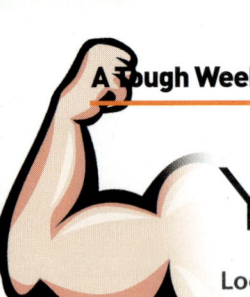

Your Energy Levels

Look at the graph of Michelle's energy levels at different times of the day. Graph your own energy levels below to show when you feel at your best. Use your graph to explain the high points and low points in your day.

> In the morning, I can concentrate on my work better than in the afternoon. After 2 p.m., my concentration drops dramatically. Then, it recovers after 5 p.m.

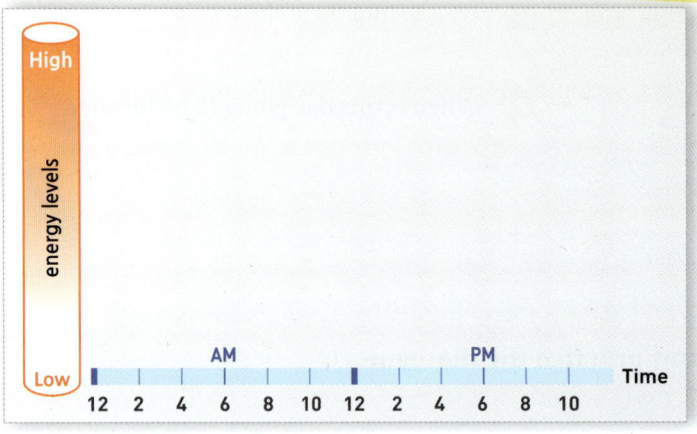

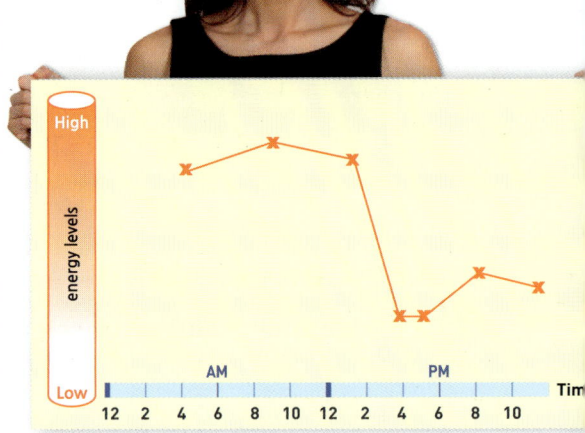

4. Language Practice

Using the key words, complete the sentences then practice making your own sentences.

Practice #1 — How is it going?

- your morning
- a good week
- your day

★ Are you having _____ _____ ?

★ How is _____ treating you so far?

★ How is _____ going?

Practice #2 — Explaining about your day

- to be over
- downhill
- a relaxing day

★ It's been _____ considering it's hump day.

★ I can't wait for this day _____ .

★ The week is all _____ after today.

Practice #3 — Giving suggestions

- knock off early
- keep your head up
- taking a longer lunch

★ How about _____ _____ today?

★ Why don't we _____ _____ today?

★ Just _____ ; the week is almost over, right?

5. Role Plays

Look at the situations and act out the role plays with your partner.

Situation #1

Role A
You meet a friend for coffee and he or she seems upset.

1. Greet your friend and ask how he or she is doing.
2. Ask your friend what is wrong.
3. Listen and then offer encouragement.

Role B
You are having a very difficult week at work and it is only Wednesday. You have fallen behind on a big project and are scared to tell your boss. Tell your friend about your problems over coffee.

1. Tell your friend you are not having a good day.
2. Describe your work problems in detail.
3. Thank your friend for listening.

Role A
It's Tuesday night and you want to invite your friend to dinner.

1. Ask your friend what they are doing tonight.
2. Offer your friend encouragement because he or she sounds stressed.
3. Offer to meet on the weekend instead.

Role B
You want to meet your friend but are too busy preparing for a big presentation that you have to give on Friday.

1. Explain you are too busy with work.
2. Say that you wish the weekend was sooner.
3. Agree to meet your friend.

Situation #2

Situational Collocations!

Look at the collocations and try making your own sentences.

stressed out	I'm so stressed out these days.
busy bee	The busy bee has no time for sorrow.
hectic schedule	I have a hectic schedule for the next few days.
time-consuming job	It is a very inconvenient and time-consuming job.
sweated blood	She sweated blood to finish the project on time.
keep up	This is too much work! I can't keep up.
steady job	My job gives me a headache at times, but I won't quit because it is a steady job.
weekend shifts	Do I get paid overtime for weekend shifts?

1.
2.

A Tough Week

Cheer Up, Buddy!

Occasionally your co-workers or friends might feel a little lost or low during the week. At times like this, you can try to cheer them up with a motivational message like the ones below. Read through the messages and think about what kinds of situations they would be appropriate for.

> "Hitch your wagon to a star."
>
> "Look on the bright side."
>
> "Love the moment, and the energy of that moment will spread beyond all boundaries."
>
> "Life is what we make it. Always has been, always will be."
>
> "I'll keep my fingers crossed for you."
>
> "There are no shortcuts to any place worth going."
>
> "You cannot step into the same river twice."
>
> "A good plan today is better than a perfect plan tomorrow."

6. Cultural Discussion Questions

Talk about the questions in as much detail as possible.

1. In your country, is it common for employees to need to finish work outside of their regular working hours? Explain.
2. Do you think that companies should let employees have flexible working schedules? Why or why not?
3. Do you feel that the rest of the week goes by faster or slower after a holiday? Explain.
4. How do you deal with stress when you are having a difficult week?

Did You Know?

Read and discuss how you feel about each fact.

1. Did you know that *June 21st* is considered *the longest day* of the year?
2. Did you know that *Tuesday* is considered *the cheapest day* to buy airline tickets?

Are You an "Early Bird" or a "Night Owl"?

An "early bird" is a "morning person" who wakes up early in the day feeling energized. They tend to become more tired as the day goes on.

"I guess I'm an early bird because I really enjoy getting up early in the morning, taking a good shower, and getting a nice early start to my day."

A "night owl" is someone who is most energetic at night. Night owls enjoy staying up late and often have trouble getting up in the morning.

"I'm definitely a night owl. I can stay up all night and be fine, but getting up early in the morning is always painful for me."

7. Slang & Idioms

Match the slang phrases and idioms with their definitions and use them to complete the sentences below.

1. ___ crunch time
2. ___ power through
3. ___ personal day
4. ___ buckle down
5. ___ slack off

A. a day of leave from work for reasons other than illness or vacation
B. to tackle a task with determination
C. a period when there's a lot of pressure to complete work quickly
D. to continue to work hard despite being tired or having difficulties
E. to work lazily

1. We can't _____ now! We're almost done.
2. The project is due tomorrow, so it's _____.
3. I'm going to take a _____ tomorrow to run some errands.
4. Even though I was sick, I had to _____ my to-do list.
5. I really need to _____ if I'm going to finish this report by 5.

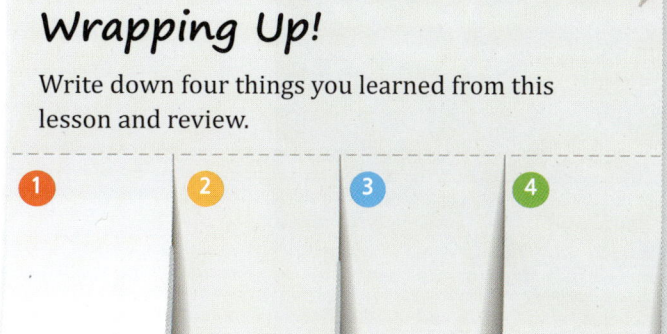

Wrapping Up!

Write down four things you learned from this lesson and review.

1
2
3
4

Streaming Trends

10

Streaming Trends

Upon completion of this lesson, you will be able to...

discuss the benefits of streaming services.

☑ Do we really need another streaming service?
☑ Does it have any unique content?
☑ How many devices can use the service at once?

1. Warm Up Activity

Describe what is happening in the picture.

Talk about the questions.

1. Do you subscribe to any streaming services?

2. What are the pros of streaming services? Are there any cons?

3. Do you prefer to watch movies at home or the movie theater?

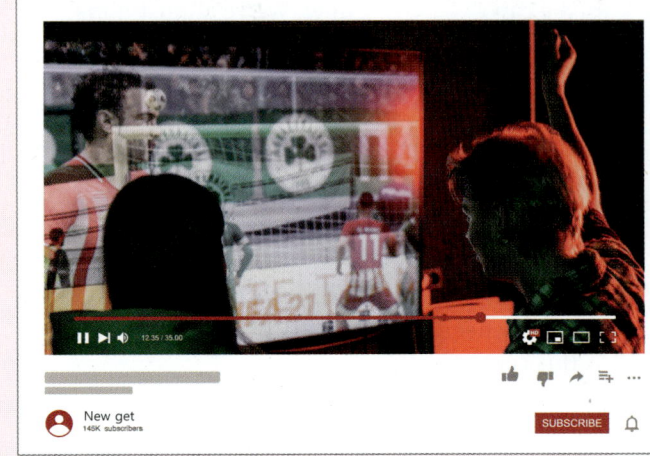

2. Useful Expressions

Match the expressions (a-d) to its similar meaning (1-4).

- **A** Can we share an account?
- **B** Does it recommend shows I might like?
- **C** How often is new content added?
- **D** People seem to love the original content.

- **1** Do they updates the content library often?
- **2** The original programming seems to be a hit.
- **3** Will the service suggest programs for me?
- **4** Can multiple people use the same account?

3. Key Conversation

🎧 Think of the useful expressions and practice the dialogue.

Let's Try It Out

Derek	Lucy, what do you think about getting Disney+?
Lucy	Do we really need another streaming service? We already have three.
Derek	Yeah, but Disney+ has the entire collection of Star Wars and Marvel movies!
Lucy	Aren't those available on the ones we already subscribe to?
Derek	There are a few but Disney+ has them all, and so much more.
Lucy	Is it really that different from what we have?
Derek	Absolutely, it has a bunch of exclusive content.
Lucy	Okay, and how much is Disney+ going to cost us?
Derek	It's pretty reasonable, and they're offering a three-month free trial!
Lucy	Fine, let's try it out and see if it's worth keeping.
Derek	Great! It'll be perfect for our family movie nights.

Questions

1. Do you think Lucy really wants to get Disney+?
2. Why does Derek suggest subscribing to Disney+?
3. What decision do Lucy and Derek finally make?
4. What changes Lucy's mind?

Streaming Trends

Look at the timeline of Netflix below.

Netflix Timeline

was founded in year **1997**	domain Netflix.com **1998**	subscription DVDs by email **1999**	+5 million subscribers **2005**	streaming service **2007**	launching in Canada **2010**
today +200 million subscribers	**2017** 100 million subscribers	**2016** available worldwide	**2013** first original series	**2012** launching in Europe	**2011** launching in Latin America

1. How has Netflix changed over time?
2. What do you think helped Netflix grow its number of subscribers?

4. Language Practice

Using the key words, complete the sentences then practice making your own sentences.

Practice #1 — Talking about features

- offline viewing
- search function
- GroupWatch feature

★ If we use the _____, we could watch our favorite shows together remotely.

★ Does it allow _____ _____?

★ The _____ really helps us find shows we like.

Practice #2 — Talking about functions

- algorithm / interests
- notifications / episodes
- create / user profiles

★ The _____ automatically recommends movies that match my _____.

★ You should _____ different _____ for each family member.

★ Turn on the _____ to get updated when new _____ come out.

Practice #3 — Confirming details

- How much does it cost?
- When does the subscription renew?
- Do we really need another streaming service?

★ A: _____ _____?
B: It's $12 a month or only $100 for a yearly subscription.

★ A: _____ _____?
B: Yes, there is so much unique content.

★ A: _____ _____?
B: It automatically renews on the 15th of each month.

5. Role Plays

Look at the situations and act out the role plays with your partner.

Situation #1

Role A

Your spouse signed up for many new streaming services recently. However, you already have three and they seem very similar to you. You rarely watch TV and would like to cancel some services.

1. Ask if you really need all the streaming services.
2. Emphasize how expensive the subscriptions are.
3. Compromise and ask to cancel only one.

Role B

You love watching new content on various streaming services. You just subscribed to a new one and are really excited to watch some new content.

1. Explain why you need different streaming services.
2. Emphasize how different the content is.
3. Agree to cancel one.

Situation #2

Role A

You went to your friend's home and found out that your friend bought a new, portable smart TV. You have been thinking about upgrading your home entertainment center, too.

1. Compliment the new smart TV.
2. Inquire about the smart TV's features, such as apps and streaming services.
3. Ask for streaming service recommendations.

Role B

Your friend came over to your new house for dinner. You show your friend around and answer questions about your new smart TV.

1. Tell your friend about why you bought it.
2. Share that your new TV came with free trials to a few streaming services.
3. Share your opinion about different streaming services.

Situational Collocations!

Look at the collocations and try making your own sentences.

watch offline	The app allows you to download shows to watch offline.
streaming quality	The streaming quality automatically adjusts based on your internet speed.
parental controls	Parental controls keep kids from watching inappropriate content.
buffering issues	A poor internet connection can cause buffering issues.
watch party	We're having a watch party for the latest episode.
device compatibility	Check device compatibility before subscribing to a new streaming service.
viewing history	You can delete items from your viewing history.
season premiere	The season premiere will be available at midnight.

1. ....
2. ....

Streaming Trends

Considering a New Streaming Service? Here's a Checklist!

Choosing a streaming service is an important decision because it affects your entertainment budget and leisure time. With so many options out there, you should think carefully before clicking "subscribe." Here are a few questions to ask yourself before committing to a new streaming service subscription.

- ☑ Does the service offer a free trial, and how long does it last?
- ☑ Can I change or cancel my subscription without extra fees?
- ☑ What are the rules about multiple users on one account?
- ☑ How often is new content added?
- ☑ Will I be able to watch on my phone, tablet, TV, or game console?
- ☑ Are there shows or movies I can't watch anywhere else?
- ☑ Does it offer HD or 4K streaming?

Q. Have you ever subscribed to a streaming service and then realized you didn't need it? What did you do?

Q. What other questions would you like to add to the list?

6. Cultural Discussion Questions

Talk about the questions in as much detail as possible.

1. Do you prefer streaming services over traditional TV broadcasts? If so, why?
2. How have streaming services changed the way people watch television in your country?
3. What are some popular streaming platforms used in your country, and why are they preferred over traditional TV?
4. What do you think of some drawbacks or disadvantages associated with streaming services?

Did You Know?

Read and discuss how you feel about each fact.

1. Did you know that the number of video streaming service users is closer to *1.8 billion as of 2023*?
2. Did you know that the top five streaming services in the U. S.—Amazon Prime, Netflix, Paramount+, Hulu and Max—with the most inclusive plans with no ads and you'll *pay about $150 a month*?

Lesson 10 / Streaming Trends **69**

Creating a **Home Cinema Experience**

High-Quality Sound System: Watching a movie is better when the sound is good. Think about getting a soundbar or speakers for great sound all over.

Lighting: Adjustable lights and dark curtains can make it feel like you're in a movie theater. You can even get smart lights that change by themselves while you watch a movie.

The Right Screen: Everyone loves a big screen. But make sure the TV ˜ts your room well and you can sit far enough away from it. A good rule is to sit about 1.5 times the TV's width away from the screen.

Seating: Make sure you have a nice place to sit. A soft couch or chairs that lean back make movie marathons very comfortable.

Q1. What do you like about watching movies at home compared to a movie theater?

Q2. Is there anything else you would add to the list?

7. Slang & Idioms

Match the slang phrases and idioms with their definitions and use them to complete the sentences below.

1. ___ reality TV junkie
2. ___ cliffhanger
3. ___ binge-watch
4. ___ screen time
5. ___ spoilers

A. the amount of time spent watching content on a screen
B. someone who is excessively fond of watching reality television shows
C. a description of a plot the may reduce surprise for a first-time viewer or reader
D. an ending that leaves the audience wanting more
E. to watch several episodes of a show In a row

1. The episode ended on such a _____. I can't wait for next season.
2. Ever since I reduced my _____, I've had more time for other hobbies.
3. Melissa is a total _____. She knows all the latest gossip about the stars.
4. When I'm stressed, I like to _____ old sitcoms.
5. Please no _____, I haven't watched the movie yet.

WRAPPING UP!

Write down four things you learned from this lesson and review.

1.
2.
3.
4.

Budgeting

11 Budgeting

» Learning Objective

Upon completion of this lesson, you will be able to...

create a monthly budget based on your needs and wants.

» Expression Check

- ☑ We need to set aside some money.
- ☑ This should be enough to cover the basic necessities.
- ☑ What's left over for savings?

1. Warm Up Activity

Describe what is happening in the picture.

Talk about the questions.

1. Would you rather save for the future or spend your money on things that make you happy now? Explain.
2. Do you think it is important to plan a budget in advance? Why or why not?
3. On an average day, how much money do you spend?

2. Useful Expressions

Match the expressions (a-d) to its similar meaning (1-4).

A I'm broke.

B Could you spot me $10 until the weekend?

C I can't afford that on my salary!

D Did you see his new car? He must be loaded!

1 Could you let me borrow some cash until Friday?

2 I don't make enough money to buy this!

3 I don't have any money.

4 He must be rich because he bought an expensive car.

3. Key Conversation

 Think of the useful expressions and practice the dialogue.

Number Crunching

Krista	I don't get it. We have money, don't we?
Eric	Krista, we need to set aside some money for our vacation.
Krista	I know, but we're not going for another month.
Eric	Yeah, but it's going to cost a lot of money. I don't know if we'll have enough to do everything we want to.
Krista	It'll be OK. We have our Visa, don't we?
Eric	I don't think putting everything on our credit card is the best idea.
Krista	Why not? We use it for everything else.
Eric	Yeah, and the interest is really starting to hurt.
Krista	OK, so we'll pay it off with our next paycheck.
Eric	OK, so what's left over for savings?
Krista	Don't worry. With my new job, we'll have enough to cover the basic necessities.

Questions

1. Who do you think is more concerned about money?
2. Do you think they will be able to afford their vacation?
3. Do you think Krista is planning enough for the future? Why or why not?
4. What would you do in this situation?

Budgeting

How to Cut Costs

Nearly 60% of respondents told us that the best way to cut costs is by cooking at home instead of eating out.

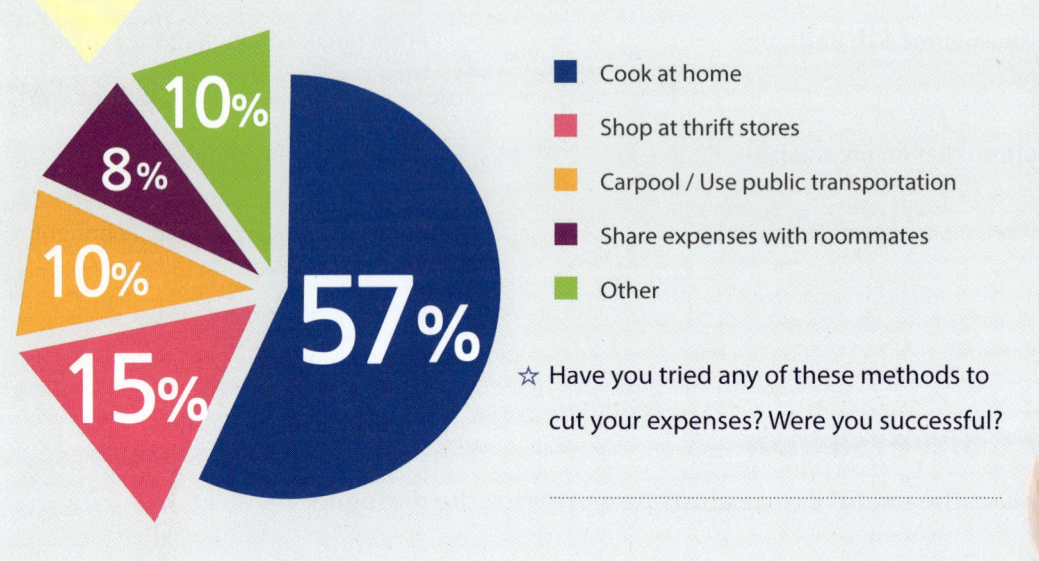

- Cook at home
- Shop at thrift stores
- Carpool / Use public transportation
- Share expenses with roommates
- Other

☆ Have you tried any of these methods to cut your expenses? Were you successful?

4. Language Practice

Using the key words, complete the sentences then practice making your own sentences.

Practice #1 — Budget planning

- $900 / rent
- $350 / groceries
- $150 / transportation

★ I think _____ should cover our _____ expenses for the month.

★ We have to budget _____ for _____.

★ We need to set aside _____ for _____.

Practice #2 — Budgeting issues

- tight budget
- making ends meet
- insufficient funds

★ I'm sorry, but you have _____ in your bank account.

★ Is he having trouble _____ _____?

★ How can we afford this on our _____?

Practice #3 — Making payments

- receipt
- expense
- income

★ Our _____ should be able to cover the cost.

★ Could I have a _____?

★ This isn't a normal monthly _____.

Lesson 11 / Budgeting   73

5. Role Plays

Look at the situations and act out the role plays with your partner.

Situation #1

Role A

You are planning a vacation with your friend. You just got a promotion and don't mind spending a little extra to go somewhere nice.

1. Ask your friend where he or she wants to go.
2. Suggest that you stay in a 5-star hotel.
3. Compromise on a reasonably priced hotel.

Role B

You want to go somewhere with your friend, but you can't afford to go on an expensive trip because you are saving for a new car.

1. Agree on a destination with your friend.
2. Explain why you don't want to spend much money on a hotel now.
3. Thank your friend for understanding.

Situation #2

Role A

You don't have money for rent. You realize you are bad at budgeting and need help from your roommate. You know your roommate will be disappointed because you have borrowed money for the last two months in a row.

1. Ask your roommate if you can borrow money until you get paid next week.
2. Apologize and ask for advice on how to manage your money better.
3. Thank your roommate and promise to follow his or her advice.

Role B

Your roommate often makes large unnecessary purchases at the beginning of the month and needs to borrow from you to pay other bills. This is the third month in a row he or she has asked to borrow from you.

1. Agree but explain why you are unhappy about the situation.
2. Give your roommate polite advice on saving money.
3. Offer to help your roommate make a budget.

Situational Collocations!

Look at the collocations and try making your own sentences.

household expenses	Managing household expenses is not an easy task.
tight budget	We traveled on a tight budget.
make payment	How do you want to make payment – cash or credit?
splashed out	I have never really splashed out on anything.
run out of money	We ran out of money and had to come home early.
steady income	Retired workers are worried that they no longer have a steady income.
pay our debt	We need to pay our debt first.
minimum wage	Many part-time job workers are paid minimum wage.

1.
2.

Budgeting

What does the expression "Money doesn't grow on trees" mean?

Learn more idioms!

* **not made of money**: to not have a lot of money
  Example) *I am not made of money,* and I do not like wasting it on stupid things.
* **pinch pennies**: to be careful with money, to be thrifty
  Example) My grandmother always **pinches pennies** and never spends her money foolishly.

Mommy, I want that toy!

Money doesn't grow on trees.

6. Cultural Discussion Questions

Talk about the questions in as much detail as possible.

1. In your country, is it common for parents to pay for all of their child's college expenses? If not, how do students usually pay?
2. Some people say that "money makes the world go round." Do you agree?
3. In your opinion, is it better for one spouse to be responsible for managing the finances or should a married couple share in the responsibility? Explain.
4. How do people usually save money in your country? Give specific examples.

Did You Know?

Read and discuss how you feel about each fact.

1. Did you know that the average American has **3.1** *credit cards*?
2. Did you know that Visa has more than **323 million** *cardholders* and it can be used in *over 8 million* locations *worldwide*?

Guess Who Spends More?

Men and women have different spending habits, spending more or less in different areas. Who do you thinks spends more?

In an average month, people in the US spend money on…

Single Men		Single Women
$139.50	GROCERIES	$133.50
$102.00	DINING OUT	$69.50
$72.00	PHONE	$54.00
$15.00	ENTERTAINMENT	$12.00
$47.00	TRAVEL	$38.50
$21.00	PERSONAL CARE	$35.50
$16.50	PETS	$23.50
$46.50	CLOTHING & SHOES	$67.00
$14.50	ELECTRONICS	$9.00
$94.50	GAS	$63.50

7. Slang & Idioms

Match the slang phrases and idioms with their definitions and use them to complete the sentences below.

1. ___ money pit
2. ___ break even
3. ___ make a dent
4. ___ side hustle
5. ___ gig economy

A. for income to equal expenses
B. a job market where temporary or freelance jobs are common
C. a job or business that one does in addition to a main job
D. something that continually requires more money for maintenance or expenses
E. to have a significant impact, especially in terms of spending or saving money

1. The new café hopes to _____ within the first year.
2. There's still a long way to go before we _____ in our fundraising goal.
3. That old car I bought has become a _____. It always needs something new repaired.
4. Many people love the freedom of the _____ because they can choose when and where to work.
5. My _____ as a graphic designer helps me pay for vacations.

Wrapping Up!

Write down four things you learned from this lesson and review.

1. _____
2. _____
3. _____
4. _____

Calling in Sick

Calling in **Sick**

12

» Learning Objective

Upon completion of this lesson, you will be able to...

provide an excuse for missing work.

» Expression Check

☑ I feel under the weather today.
☑ I think I'm coming down with something.
☑ I need to call in sick today.

1. Warm Up Activity

Describe what is happening in the picture.

Talk about the questions.

1. Have you ever been so sick that you could not go to work?
2. What is your company's policy regarding sick days?
3. Do you feel that it is acceptable to call in sick for minor illnesses? Explain.

2. Useful Expressions

Match the expressions (a-d) to its similar meaning (1-4).

A I feel under the weather today.

B I think I'm coming down with something.

C I need to use one of my sick days.

D I think I'm contagious.

1 If other people are around me, they might get sick, too.

2 I think I feel a cold coming on.

3 I think I'm going to be sick.

4 I need to call in sick today.

3. Key Conversation

🎧 Think of the useful expressions and practice the dialogue.

A Day to Rest

Mary	Hi Brad. I don't think I'll be able to make it into work today.
Brad	Oh? Why not?
Mary	I feel kind of under the weather today. I think I came down with something over the weekend.
Brad	That's too bad. Should I send someone over to check up on you?
Mary	No, I don't think so. I might be contagious.
Brad	Good point. Well, we all hope you feel better soon.
Mary	Yeah, I'm really sorry. I know we have that big project that is due tomorrow.
Brad	Don't worry about that. Just stay at home and rest. I'll have Rebecca take care of it.
Mary	Are you sure? I feel really bad for letting the team down.
Brad	Like I said, take a day to rest. You won't be any good to us if you're sick.

Questions

1. Who do you think Brad is?
2. Why doesn't Mary want someone to check on her?
3. Do you think Rebecca will be upset about doing Mary's work?
4. Do you think Mary should stay home and rest or go into her office to do her work?

Calling in Sick

Various Excuses for Calling in Sick

Many people call in sick because of a cold or flu. However, calling off work for "just a cold" can be seen as a sign of weakness at work. Sometimes, you might be tempted to tell a little <u>white lie</u> to make a more convincing excuse.

> White lies are minor lies which could be considered to be harmless, or even beneficial, in the long term.
>
> For example, pretend that a friend or family member cooked for you. You do not really like the food, but you know he spent time and effort making it for you. So, when he asks how it is, you tell a white lie and say that it tastes great.

CareerBuilder conducted a survey of over 5,000 workers and employers and discovered the top 11 weirdest reasons reasons people have used when calling in sick.

Unusual Excuses for Calling in Sick

1. Employee said a chicken attacked his mom.
2. Employee's finger was stuck in a bowling ball.
3. Employee had a hair transplant gone bad.
4. Employee fell asleep at his desk while working and hit his head.
5. Employee said a cow broke into her house.
6. Employee's girlfriend threw a Sit'n Spin through his living room window.
7. Employee's foot was caught in the garbage disposal.
8. Employee called in sick from a bar at 5:00 p.m. the night before.
9. Employee said he was not feeling too clever that day.
10. Employee had to mow the lawn to avoid a lawsuit.
11. Employee called in the day after Thanksgiving because she burned her mouth on pumpkin pie.

4. Language Practice

Using the key words, complete the sentences then practice making your own sentences.

Practice #1 — Describing feelings	Practice #2 — Describing sickness	Practice #3 — Describing symptoms
• caught something • under the weather • coming down with something	• have / headache • throat / sore • nose / running	• It hurts when I swallow. • I feel pain in my chest. • I feel nauseous.
★ I'm feeling _____ right now. ★ I think I'm _____ _____ . ★ I think I _____ last weekend.	★ My _____ is very _____ today. ★ My _____ is _____ like crazy. ★ I _____ a very bad _____ .	★ A: _____. B: You probably have food poisoning. ★ A: _____. B: That sounds like a sore throat. ★ A: _____. B: I think you have heartburn.

5. Role Plays

Look at the situations and act out the role plays with your partner.

Situation #1

Role A

You are in bed sick with the flu. Call your supervisor to let him or her know you won't be coming in today.

1. Apologize for calling so early and explain you are sick.
2. Describe your symptoms to your supervisor.
3. Apologize for not coming in.

Role B

You are a team leader at an office. You are at home getting ready for work when your phone rings.

1. Ask about their illness.
2. Express regret that he or she is not feeling well.
3. Tell your employee not to worry and to focus on getting better.

Situation #2

Role A

You woke up with a case of severe food poisoning and are too sick to work. However, you were supposed to deliver a presentation today. Call a co-worker and ask him or her to cover for you.

1. Tell your co-worker about your situation.
2. Ask if your co-worker can present the material for you.
3. Thank him or her for the help.

Role B

Your team is preparing for a presentation today. Your task was making the PowerPoint. You are familiar with the material.

1. Answer the call.
2. Say that it is no problem.
3. Tell your co-worker that you hope he or she feels better and end the call.

Situational Collocations!

Look at the collocations and try making your own sentences.

look off-color	You look a little off-color today. Are you ill?
take a sick leave	I need to take a sick leave; my cold is getting worse by the minute.
get car-sick	I get car-sick if I sit in the back seat.
upset stomach	I have an upset stomach, maybe it was from dinner.
emergency room	My mom was rushed to the emergency room this morning.
chronic pain	He has had chronic pain in his back for years.
kick back and relax	Why don't you just kick back and relax at home?
concerned for	I'm a bit concerned for your health.

1. ....
2. ....

Calling in Sick

Texting in Sick

When it comes to notifying employers that they are taking a sick day, some workers have reported they are bypassing a phone call to the boss and relying on digital communication.

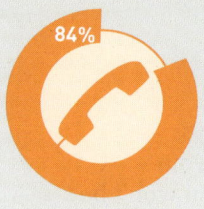  

Phone call **84%** E-mail **24%** Text message **11%**

Checking Up on Employees

Calling in sick without a reasonable excuse can result in serious consequences like getting fired. According to a survey, employers responded that they have checked up on employees in various ways, citing the examples on the chart.

- 16% drove by the employee's home
- 19% had another employee call the employee
- 52% called the employee
- 69% required a doctor's note

6. Cultural Discussion Questions

Talk about the questions in as much detail as possible.

1. In some countries, it is common for parents to stay home when their children are sick. How about yours?

2. In your country, do most people go to the doctor for minor symptoms or do they wait until they are very sick? Explain.

3. What would happen in your company if someone was caught lying about being sick to enjoy a paid day off?

4. Tell about the last time you called in sick. Who did you call? What did you say?

Did You Know?

Read and discuss how you feel about each fact.

1. Did you know that most people who get the influenza (flu) virus become sick *between October and May*?

2. Did you know that all EU countries require companies to give their employees a *minimum of 20 sick days a year*?

DOs & DON'Ts

- If you start feeling sick while at work, **DO** make sure you mention it to the boss.
- If illness strikes over the weekend or in the evening, **DO** call in by the prescribed time on the next working day.
- If you think you may have something contagious, **DO** get a medical confirmation as quickly as possible and inform your workplace straight away.

As for the Don'ts, these are simple:

- **DON'T** call in sick when you are perfectly well and just want a day off. Your co-workers will not thank you for their increased workload, and you are unlikely to get any sympathy if you become ill later.
- **DON'T** call in sick and then go shopping in town that afternoon. Even if you were genuinely feeling ill in the morning, no one will believe you. If you are seen by your manager or boss, you will be in trouble the next day.

7. Slang & Idioms

Match the slang phrases and idioms with their definitions and use them to complete the sentences below.

1. ___ out of commission
2. ___ wiped out
3. ___ splitting headache
4. ___ couldn't keep anything down
5. ___ took a turn for the worse

A. a very bad pain in your head
B. extremely tired or drained
C. temporarily unable to work or perform activities due to sickness
D. to become sick again after seeming to get better
E. to throw up all you eat

1. By the end of the hike, we were completely _____.
2. The loud music at the party gave me a _____.
3. Emily's stomach bug was so bad that she _____.
4. The patient was stable, but suddenly, their condition _____.
5. Jake's back injury has left him _____. We'll have to find someone to replace him for the next game.

Wrapping Up!

Write down four things you learned from this lesson and review.

New Get Up To Speed+ Book 1
SLANG & IDIOM GLOSSARY

Lesson 1

vibes with	to have a good understanding or to be on the same wavelength
sees eye to eye	to agree with someone
tight	to be in a very close relationship or friendship
in sync	to work well together, in harmony
click	to quickly get along well with someone

Lesson 2

hang out	to spend time with someone socially
make a day of it	to devote a whole day to an activity
tag along	to accompany someone to a place or event
short notice	having only a brief time to prepare for something
grabbing a coffee	to meet to drink coffee

Lesson 3

on point	looking very well put-together and styled
off day	a day when someone doesn't look or feel their best
bed head	the messy appearance of a person's hair after first waking up
glow up	a positive physical transformation
definite upgrade	a clear and noticeable improvement

Lesson 4

to-go box	a container used by a restaurant customer to take home leftover food
bit off more than I can chew	to take on a task that is way too big
to die for	to be exceptionally good or desirable
can really pack it away	to be able to eat a lot
worked up an appetite	to do something so difficult that it makes you hungry

Lesson 5

stepped up	to take responsibility, especially in a challenging situation
in my element	feeling comfortable in an environment or activity
not my scene	not something one enjoys or is interested in
keeps it real	stays true to oneself, honest, and authentic
goes the extra mile	does more than what is expected or required

Lesson 6

separate checks	individual bills for each customer in a group
got yours	to cover someone else's portion of a bill
split the check	to divide up a bill
settle up	to pay what's owed
good for it	can be trusted to repay a debt

Lesson 7

go dark	when someone is not reachable via electronic means or social media
sync up	to link data across devices or accounts
hard reset	returning a device to its original factory settings
digital detox	a period of time when a person stops using electronic devices
doomscrolling	obsessively checking for updates with the expectation that the news will be bad

Lesson 8

runs in the family	to be hereditary
come down with	to begin to suffer from an illness
clean bill of health	fit and healthy
fighting off something	recovering from an illness
in the clear	no longer affected by or at risk of a particular illness

Lesson 9

crunch time	a period when there's a lot of pressure to complete work quickly
power through	to continue to work hard despite being tired or having difficulties
personal day	a day of leave from work for reasons other than illness or vacation
buckle down	to tackle a task with determination
slack off	to work lazily

Lesson 10

reality TV junkie	someone who is excessively fond of watching reality television shows
cliffhanger	an ending that leaves the audience wanting more
binge-watch	to watch several episodes of a show In a row
screen time	the amount of time spent watching content on a screen
spoilers	a description of a plot the may reduce surprise for a first-time viewer or reader

Lesson 11

money pit	something that continually requires more money for maintenance or expenses
break even	for income to equal expenses
make a dent	to have a significant impact, especially in terms of spending or saving money
side hustle	a job or business that one does in addition to a main job
gig economy	a job market where temporary or freelance jobs are common

Lesson 12

out of commission	temporarily unable to work or perform activities due to sickness
wiped out	extremely tired or drained
splitting headache	a very bad pain in your head
couldn't keep anything down	to throw up all you eat
took a turn for the worse	to become sick again after seeming to get better

New Get Up To Speed+ Book 1
ANSWER KEY

Lesson 1

Useful Expressions

a 3
b 4
c 2
d 1

Language Practice

Practice #1
- a co-worker
- my new boyfriend/girlfriend
- my old friend

Practice #2
- glad to meet you
- finally meet
- a pleasure to meet

Practice #3
- have heard / about
- put a face
- talks about / all the time

Slang & Idioms

1 D tight
2 B in sync
3 A vibes with
4 C click
5 E sees eye to eye

Lesson 2

Useful Expressions

a 2
b 4
c 1
d 3

Language Practice

Practice #1
- watch / on TV
- go hiking / Saturday
- go shopping / tomorrow

Practice #2
- all
- all
- all

Practice #3
- go skiing
- movie marathon
- having dinner

Slang & Idioms

1 E tag along
2 A hang out
3 B grabbing a coffee
4 C short notice
5 D make a day of it

Lesson 3

Useful Expressions

a 3
b 1
c 4
d 2

Language Practice

Practice #1
- a few inches / off
- layers
- trim

Practice #2
- adding highlights
- cover up the gray
- touch up my roots

Practice #3
★ sideburns
★ shave the back of my neck
★ bangs

Slang & Idioms
1	C	bed head
2	B	glow up
3	D	on point
4	A	definite upgrade
5	E	off day

Lesson 4

Useful Expressions
a	3
b	4
c	2
d	1

Language Practice

Practice #1
★ all
★ all
★ all

Practice #2
★ dessert / fudge brownie
★ drink / draft beer
★ appetizer / garden salad

Practice #3
★ new Italian place
★ all
★ fast food restaurant

Slang & Idioms
1	A	bit off more than I can chew;
2	E	to die for
3	B	to-go box
4	C	can really pack it away
5	D	worked up an appetite

Lesson 5

Useful Expressions
a	4
b	1
c	2
d	3

Language Practice

Practice #1
★ going grocery shopping
★ set the table
★ clean the living room

Practice #2
★ all
★ all
★ all

Practice #3
★ all
★ all
★ all

Slang & Idioms
1	E	not my scene
2	C	keeps it real
3	A	in my element
4	B	stepped up
5	D	went the extra mile

Lesson 6

Useful Expressions
a	3
b	4
c	1
d	2

New Get Up To Speed+ Book 1
ANSWER KEY

Language Practice

Practice #1
★ dinner is on me
★ take care of the check
★ pick up the tab

Practice #2
★ last week / tonight
★ yesterday / this morning
★ lunch / dinner / me

Practice #3
★ got it or took care of the bill
★ treat me
★ took care of the bill

Slang & Idioms

1	C	got yours
2	E	settle up
3	A	separate checks
4	B	good for it
5	D	split the check

Lesson 7

Useful Expressions

a	3
b	4
c	2
d	1

Language Practice

Practice #1
★ all
★ wireless earbuds or Bluetooth speakers
★ all

Practice #2
★ screen resolution
★ laptop
★ battery life

Practice #3
★ fast charger or wireless charger
★ fast charger or wireless charger
★ memory

Slang & Idioms

1	E	hard reset
2	A	digital detox
3	B	sync up
4	C	doomscrolling
5	D	go dark

Lesson 8

Useful Expressions

a	3
b	2
c	4
d	1

Language Practice

Practice #1
★ back on your feet before long
★ recovery soon
★ looking / better / last weekend

Practice #2
★ diagnosis
★ recovery period
★ discharged

Practice #3
★ wishes he could be here
★ coworkers / get well
★ classmates / on the up and up

Slang & Idioms

| 1 | B | clean bill of health |
| 2 | D | fighting off something |

3	E	in the clear
4	A	runs in the family
5	C	come down with

Lesson 9

Useful Expressions

a	3
b	4
c	1
d	2

Language Practice

Practice #1
- a good week
- your day
- your morning

Practice #2
- a relaxing day
- to be over
- downhill

Practice #3
- taking a longer lunch
- knock off early
- keep your head up

Slang & Idioms

1	C	slack off
2	D	crunch time
3	A	personal day
4	B	power through
5	E	buckle down

Lesson 10

Useful Expressions

a	4
b	3
c	1
d	2

Language Practice

Practice #1
- GroupWatch feature
- offline viewing
- search function

Practice #2
- search / genre
- create / user profiles
- notifications / episodes

Practice #3
- How much does it cost?
- Do we really need another streaming service?
- When does the subscription renew?

Slang & Idioms

1	B	cliffhanger
2	D	screen time
3	E	reality TV junkie
4	A	binge-watch
5	C	spoilers

Lesson 11

Useful Expressions

a	3
b	1
c	2
d	4

Language Practice

Practice #1
- $150 / transportation
- $350 / groceries
- $900 / rent

Practice #2

New Get Up To Speed+ Book 1
ANSWER KEY

- insufficient funds
- making ends meet
- tight budget

Practice #3
- income
- receipt
- expense

Slang & Idioms

1	D	break even
2	A	make a dent
3	E	money pit
4	C	gig economy
5	B	side hustle

1	C	wiped out
2	B	splitting headache
3	A	couldn't keep anything down
4	E	took a turn for the worse
5	D	out of commission

Lesson 12

Useful Expressions

a	3
b	2
c	4
d	1

Language Practice

Practice #1
- under the weather
- coming down with something
- caught something

Practice #2
- throat / sore
- nose / running
- have / headache

Practice #3
- I feel nauseous.
- It hurts when I swallow.
- I feel pain in my chest.

Slang & Idioms